Chapter 1

Introducing Android

Google's Android has been a huge hit with consumers since its release, and in this chapter we take a brief look at the operating system's history and the different versions on offer. We also examine why you should choose an Android device over the alternatives, as well as the best-looking accessories on the market. >

Android versions

Successive versions of Android build on its open-source strengths

Perhaps one of the first questions you're likely to have about Android, is why Google gave it this name. In fact, the search giant didn't. Android was the name of a company Google bought in 2005.

Android Inc wasn't a smartphone company, nor – at that time – even one that made software to run smartphones. It was a startup founded on the premise that there was scope for a new type of smartphone that was location-aware and could be customised to the user's needs and preferences.

If you'd heard anything of Android and the people behind it, it would have been because its founder was also behind Danger Inc, the company that made the Sidekick phone for teens.

It wasn't until 2008 that Google was ready to unveil its first Android-based device, but by that stage it was an open secret that it was to be a new smartphone platform. Reading through press reports from that time, there seems to have been little inkling of just how ground-breaking this mobile operating system might be.

HTC's G1 was the first Android device to hit the market

APPLE ALTERNATIVE

That Google wanted to create a bold alternative to the Apple iPhone was clear; but Google had far greater vision than that. Behind the scenes it had begun working with the Open Handset Alliance, a consortium of 47 hardware, software and telecoms companies with the open-source Linux kernel in common. Android first went public in late 2007, with the first Android device, the G1, reaching the market in November 2008. The hardware was provided by HTC, the longest-established portable mobile device maker around and still one of the most highly regarded brands.

What was immediately clear was that Android was no rough-and-ready attempt to do something a little bit different with a subtly enhanced look. The interface was clear and uncluttered, while the navigation was fast and to the point. Connectivity was a given, as was the web and GPS location information. It just worked. Overnight, the phone in your pocket went from a useful means of contact to an indispensable information and navigation companion. By late 2009, Android devices represented the fastest growth area for phones. Even Nokia, itself

based on the open-source Symbian OS, has had to lick its wounds and retreat from its seemingly unassailable position as the king of the smartphones and into the protective arms of Microsoft.

WHICH ANDROID ARE YOU?

It's not just the appeal of the new that has led to Android's success, of course. As well as the alacrity of take-up of these new, untested Android devices, the speed of development has been a big factor. Less than a year after the original G1 handset was launched, Google had unveiled – and its hardware partners started producing – two new generations of Android smartphones. It also began giving them tasty-sounding, but un-Android-like, names.

Android 1.5 was known as Cupcake and brought to the party video capture and direct uploads to (Google-owned) video-sharing site YouTube. Entertainment also got a boost in the form of support for Bluetooth A2DP, so you could bounce music stored on your Android phone to Bluetooth wireless speakers or listen privately with Bluetooth earphones or a speakerphone. Web browsing has improved with support for cut and paste – something that's become increasingly important as we share content and links on social networks such as Twitter.

Donut (Android 1.6) was notable for its improved on-device search functions and introduced voice search for the first time. If this feature is of note, the faster hardware and better attenuation of later Android versions is worth hanging out for. The launch of Donut also saw the second big handset hit for HTC in the form of the Desire. The first 'budget' Android device, it quickly became a bestseller and brought with it a new focus on apps and customisation. From this point on in Android's development photo and video galleries were combined, so you could casually flick through whatever visual content you'd saved, but internal storage remained cramped. Surprisingly, there are still a fair few version 1.6 ›

▲ Android version 2.3 'Gingerbread' will be available on the next generation of handsets, such as the Google Nexus S

Market forces

The open-source principles of Android mean you aren't restricted to getting your apps from the Android Market, and there are several alternatives. You can also download some apps direct from the makers' websites. But you should be aware that the very nature of an open platform leaves your device vulnerable to alteration.

Android apps should inform you before you proceed to the payment (if applicable) and download process of the hardware and code to which they require access, giving you an indication of what's being exposed. Pay particular attention to this information when downloading from an independent or unverified site, and consider installing security software such as BullGuard or McAfee WaveSecure.

smartphones on the market, so check what you're getting.

Next came Eclair (confusingly known as both Android 2.0 and 2.1) in late 2010. Sideloading apps, music and video were now supported, while battery management was given a big boost. Google's own souped-up Nexus behemoth was supposed to be the poster child for the Android Market but never quite took off – not least because customers realised they could get perfectly speedy hardware running the same or nearly the same version of Android without paying the premium the Nexus demanded. In fact the ultra-desirable Samsung Galaxy S (page 144) running Android 2.1 scooped it to become 2010's device of choice.

ANDROID MARKET TAKES OFF

The Android Market nonetheless began to take off, though as owners of Eclair smartphones will be all too aware, direct support for the Market is not a given on this generation of devices. For this, you need to look to a 2.2 Froyo device .

It's also important if you want to be able to upgrade your device at some stage. Depending on whether you have a plain vanilla Android device or one that has been 'skinned' by the operator or handset manufacturer, you may find the DIY upgrade process a painful experience.

Android 2.2 is probably the most popular version of the operating system as we write. It offers direct, over the air updates to new versions of the interface as they become available, as well as incremental feature and security updates you may choose to install. The cameras now all sport flash and digital zoom, and cameraphones such as the Sony Ericsson Xperia X10 (page 146) and HTC Incredible S (page 122) with 8Mp sensors apiece provide ample reason to fork out for a premium handset.

A leap in hardware from the 400MHz or so of the Cupcake handsets to the 800MHz and 1GHz CPU on which most

Froyo devices run means multitasking and background services are now fairly seamless. Root errors, screen lock-ups and general navigation issues are now few and far between. Besides, a permanent inclusion on the Settings menu now lets you manage apps, view available storage and turn off background services such as Wi-Fi or 3G. Standby is now the biggest battery drain.

Gingerbread (Android 2.3) offers marginal improvements over Froyo, but is not so different you should discount a 2.2 device from your shortlist. With the timescales for upgrades bandied about by various operators and handset makers, you may even find a seemingly elderly, soon-to-be-a-year-old smartphone such as the Samsung Galaxy S gets a sudden boost from 2.1 to 2.3.

THE NEXT BIG THING

Aside from yet faster processing and improved Google Maps and web browsing, Gingerbread offers one notable feature upgrade – NFC (near field communications). As with the QR codes before it (and dotted about this book), it's a technology awaiting its moment in the spotlight. When it arrives, NFC will be a boon for contactless, easy payments and ticketing.

Of course, what Google was really working on at the end of 2010 and into 2011 was Honeycomb, its first operating system for tablets. Conscious that Eclair and Froyo had not transitioned perfectly in their journey from the sub-4in screen of smartphones to the 5in to 10in displays of tablets, Google has ensured the hardware and graphics acceleration are there for its first 'proper' challenge to the iPad.

The Motorola Xoom, reviewed on page 152, is a great cheerleader for Honeycomb, with a 1GHz dual-core processor under the hood and 1GB of onboard RAM. It's fast, easy to navigate and can keep up with your excitement as you flit about the screen.

Already, rival Honeycomb tablets, such as the Acer Iconia, with yet faster processors, tighter screen resolutions and more adept graphics handling are on their way. If you can contain your excitement over Honeycomb's arrival, expect more compelling – and potentially cheaper – Android tablets to march triumphantly into the shops and straight off the shelves later this year.

▲ **The Acer Iconia A500 is one of the first devices to come with Android 3.0, which was designed for tablets**

Why choose Android

With so many alternatives what does Android have to offer?

Google's mobile operating system has proven to be a big hit since it was launched back in 2008. However, there are a growing number of alternatives hitting the market, such as HP's WebOS and the BlackBerry Tablet OS. And let's not forget Apple's iOS. So why choose an Android device?

For starters, the operating system is hugely appealing to both handset manufacturers and software developers; the former because they can create their own 'skinned' version of Android, while the latter can get their apps onto the Android Market with the minimum of fuss. Anyone who wants to sell an app on iTunes needs to get it approved by Apple first. And because there's such a wide range of Android devices and apps, the operating system is proving a hit with consumers too.

THE HARDWARE

Back in 2008, Nokia declared that the smartphone was today's computer. While that claim may have stretched the imagination, even back then it wasn't a huge overstatement. Processing power is now up to 1GHz with the nVidia Tegra 2 chip, while quad-core processing, 3D video gaming and the ability to output a whole Blu-ray movie stored on a microSD card and show it on a vast silver screen are all mooted.

The Motorola Atrix handset has 16GB of internal memory and can take another 32GB via a microSD card. Remember when laptops first began touting

Motorola's Xoom runs Android 3.0, which was designed for tablets

gigabytes of storage? It's only about five years since dual-core computing arrived, yet smartphones already have dual- and even quad-core chips.

Features such as HD video-out and real-time 3D processing and output were showcased at Mobile World Congress in Barcelona in February.

While all this rich multimedia is staggeringly impressive, for the most part it's not the primary reason why you might choose a particular device in the first place. Most of us would sooner have a dependable phone that allows us to make clear calls, easily access our contacts and call, text or email them, than plump for a really fancy gadget on which calling and connectivity take a back seat.

Similarly, an impressively large or bright screen may not be the best choice if you're unlikely to be able to give your smartphone daily mains-power sustenance. These multimedia showcases require an awful lot of power, despite what smartphone chip makers say. And while you may occasionally want to kick back and catch up on the latest episode of *Spooks* on the Android version of the BBC iPlayer, that shiny 4in touchscreen needs powering every moment that the device is switched on and in active use, even if you're just having a chat via text or jotting down a note for later.

In general, a 600MHz or faster processor, expandable storage, a capacitive touchscreen – with or without a separate slide-out keypad – and 512MB of RAM will be your basic hardware requirements. A 3.5in screen with a WVGA resolution of 800x480 pixels should suffice. Check the actual pixel resolution rather than the screen size – VGA resolution on a large 3.8in-plus display will not be crisp, and may look blocky. It's worth visiting your local phone shop and comparing screen for screen – there's a big variation in quality.

A touchscreen with a zoom in/out on-screen slider is a given, but multitouch gives you more navigation control – and will drain the battery faster, too. If you're torn between two similar handsets, the one with the higher mAh battery rating will usually provide more power, so should last longer. However, some

›

The news and weather widget on Google's Nexus S

HTC has a 'skin' for Android called HTC Sense

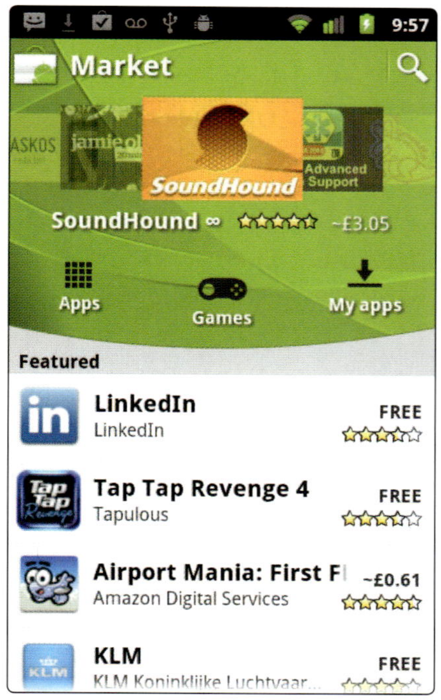

The Android Market is where you buy new apps

smartphone makers do a better job than others of battery management. On Android phones the device settings can be adjusted as you please.

Look for 802.11n Wi-Fi; 3G is useful only if you live in an area where there's solid coverage – consult maps for your area at the respective network operator's website. There are also now defined data-usage limits in place for most 3G contracts, so be mindful of this when choosing your contract and deciding whether 3G is for you.

Most Android 2.1 phones come with 5Mp cameras or better, and some can take better video than others. A VGA-resolution video mode is fine for conducting web chats, but it won't bear muster on even a laptop screen. If you're likely to want to do more than watch your footage on your smartphone or in a browser window on YouTube, choose a handset that offers 720p (HD) video capture. Some offer 1080p (full-HD) video, but this remains a luxury feature.

PLAIN OR FANCY?

As we briefly mentioned earlier one of Android's advantages is that the operating system can be 'skinned'. This means that handset manufacturers can not only change the overall look of icons, but also decide which apps will appear on the home screens. They can also change how many home screens are on offer – an unskinned version of Android has five, whereas HTC increases this to seven.

The Taiwanese company has one of the most highly regarded third-party skins in its HTC Sense. This includes a

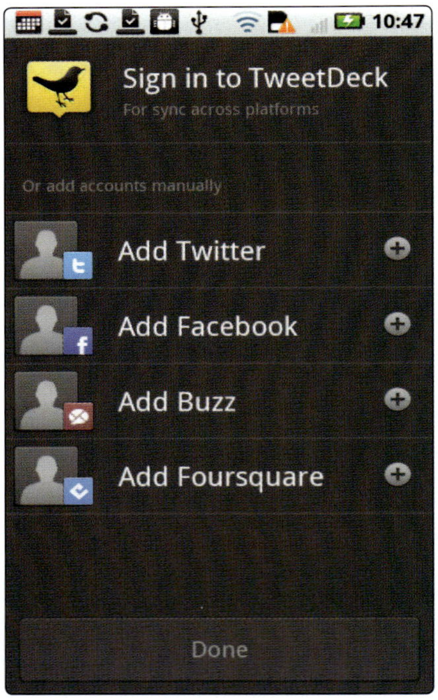

▲ TweetDeck brings your social networks together

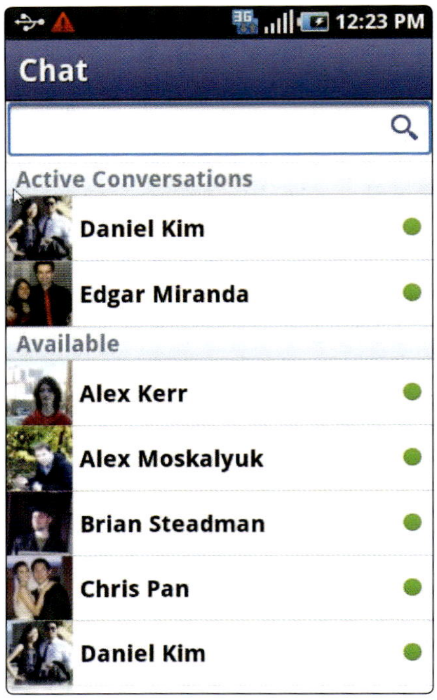

▲ Facebook helps you keep in touch with friends

▲ Android is perfect for surfing the internet

popular weather widget that can provide the temperature and a weather outlook for the home screen. This includes animations that, while they don't actually add to the information content, do add to the wow factor.

By comparison, the weather widget that's provided on the Google Nexus S (shown left) is a fairly dull and staid affair, though it does display news headlines.

MARKET MATTERS

This brings us on to one of Android's main attractions. If you don't like a particular app or widget, you can get hold of another from the Android Market.

This is Google's equivalent to the iTunes store and is packed full of apps. There is, however, an important point that you need to bear in mind. While the Android Market comes pre-installed on all smartphones, it isn't available on every tablet, such as the Advent Vega. You, therefore, need to double-check with the retailer before you purchase a tablet.

Another point to remember is that early versions of Android were designed for use on smartphones and not for devices with larger screens. This means that tablet owners won't be able to download some apps. However, with the release of Android 3.0 (Honeycomb), which was designed specifically for tablets, there are a growing number of apps that can be used on tablets.

ALL ABOUT FRIENDS

Any smartphone needs to be able to keep you in contact with your friends, and these days that means not just by voice ›

and text, but also by using things such as mobile email and social networking. Your Android device will have mobile email capability built in, and you'll be able to use this and any social networking apps either with a SIM or Wi-Fi to get regular updates.

Setting up mobile email is easy. Gmail is handled separately from other email, and after you've entered your address and password, your Gmail account will automatically sync with your Android device.

Both personal POP and IMAP email and Microsoft Exchange (work based) email is also supported and you can set up multiple accounts. You may need some login information (SMTP and POP servers for personal email), but that's easily obtained from your email address provider if you don't have it to hand.

Your Android device may come with social networking apps, such as Twitter and Facebook, built in. You can also put widgets, such as TweetDeck, on a home screen to help you stay in touch.

PHOTOGRAPHY

Back in the old days when phones weren't as smart as they are now, photography was an important aspect of mobile phones, with the ability to take a snap and send an MMS a key feature of handsets. That remains the case, but Android smartphones often now provide a 5Mp camera, some even have 8Mp on offer,

▲ Android lets you watch video that is embedded into web pages

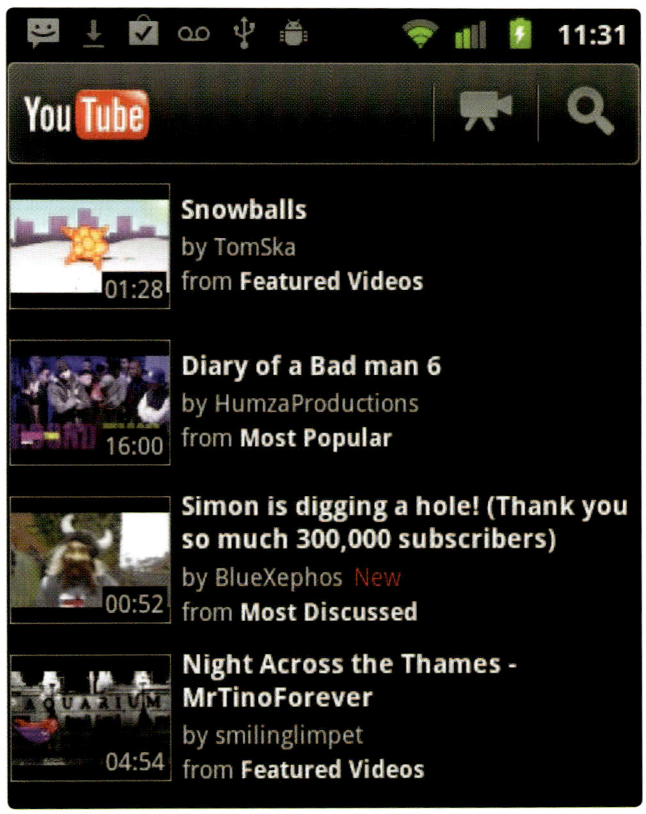

▲ Android smartphones and tablets often come with a YouTube client pre-installed

and 720p video is increasingly available. With these improvements come the ability to share photos wirelessly via DLNA, upload direct to services lick Facebook, Picasa, Flickr and YouTube, attach photos to email and, of course to edit on the device before you do any of those things.

The big screens of smartphones and tablets lend themselves to slideshows, so that they are a good place to store and view photos you have snapped.

GPS AND NAVIGATION

Something that's a strong feature of smartphones is GPS. It's not so widespread in tablets, but it is in some, for example the Samsung Galaxy Tab. This lets you use location information in apps such as Google Maps for navigations. And there are more alternatives too.

APPS GALORE

We've mentioned apps and they are a key feature of Google Android. With the caveat already noted that you need to check out your chosen Android tablet to find out about its app support, we think that apps are a key reason for choosing an Android smartphone or tablet over the competition.

Other operating systems may have apps on offer, but Android benefits from literally thousands that are free, so you can experiment and find out what suits you best.

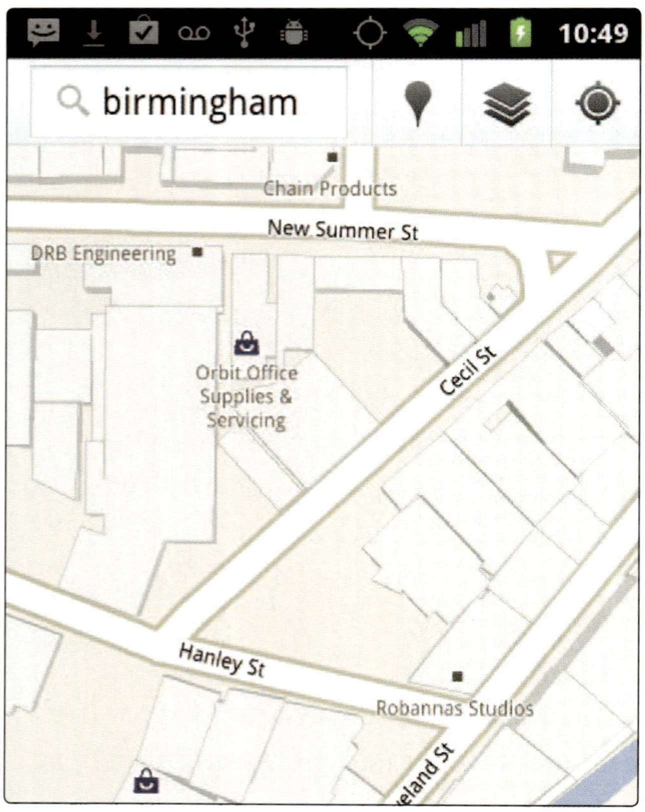

Google Maps is a staple of Android and comes as a standard feature

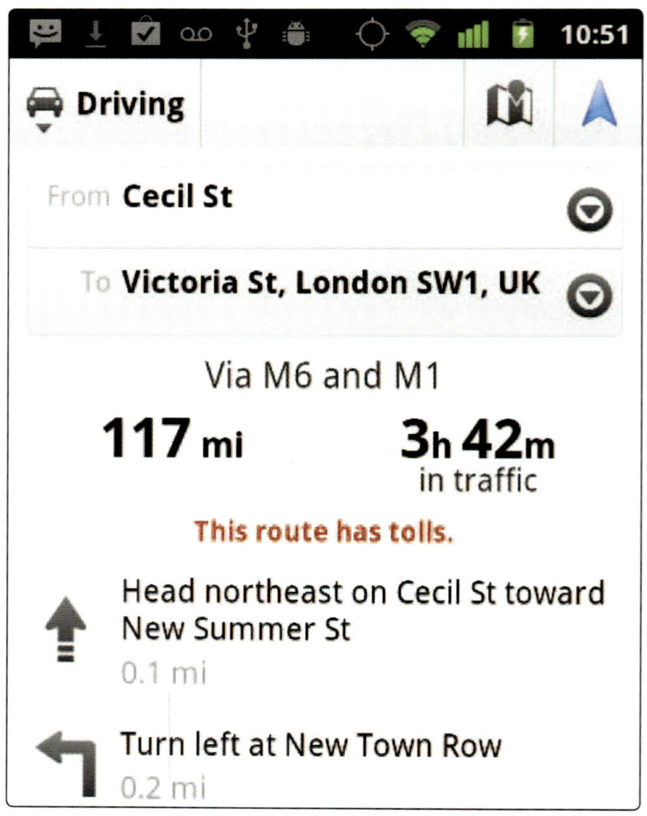

With built in GPS, you can use Google Maps for navigation

Android accessories

Whether you want to jazz up the look of your smartphone or tablet, protect its beautiful lines or add to its already considerable capabilities, there are some great-looking gadgets built just for Android

▲ JAYBIRD SPORTSBAND 2

£99; www.advancedmp3players.co.uk

These Jaybird Bluetooth headphones are some of the loveliest wire-free sets we've encountered. The sturdy-but-slim headband, well thought out controls for accepting calls and adjusting the volume and the comfort of the cushioning that rests against the head all appeal. A choice of nine colours is also available.

▼ SONOS MULTI-ROOM MUSIC PLAYER

Base controller £349; extra modules from £79 each; Android app free; www.sonos.com

If you like to have music wherever you go and to be able to change the track or the volume, this high-tech, high-fidelity marvel is one of the swankiest options around. And you can use your Android phone as a controller.

► ECHOSTAR HDR-600RS

£349; www.myechostar.com

This Echostar media-streaming box uses Slingbox's 'location-shifting' concept to send footage from your PVR or a media hard drive to your Android phone or tablet. Up to 150 channels can be viewed, so you use the Echostar to access live programmes you wouldn't otherwise be able to tune in to. You'll need the £18.16 SlingPlayer Mobile app, too.

◄ CASE MATE VENTURE

$39; www.case-mate.com

Case Mate has designed some smart cases for the Dell Streak 7 and the Samsung Galaxy Tab. These denim-style folio cases are cleverly designed to act as a stand for the tablet, as well as protecting it from wear and tear.

▼ FREELOADER CLASSIC

£39; www.solartechnology.co.uk

The Freeloader Classic is a more powerful version of a solar charger. Though not limited to Android devices, its mini USB connection means it will work with any handset that uses such a connection. The Classic has a 1200mAh battery as well as 50mAh crystalline solar cells to soak up the rays.

▶ HAUPPAUGE BROADWAY 2T

£299; www.hauppauge.co.uk

Turn your Android tablet into a portable TV by adding a wireless TV receiver. The Hauppauge Broadway 2T works with tablets and laptops, and simply requires a Wi-Fi or 3G connection over which to stream live TV programmes. Hauppauge is touting the ability to work with iPads and iPhones, but Android, Windows and Mac laptops and tablets are all supported.

▶ POWERMAT 2X WITH POWERCUBE

From $59; www.powermat.com

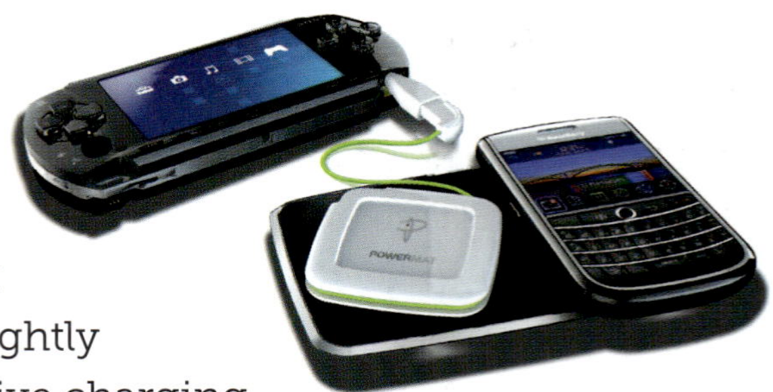

Powermat recently unveiled more wireless chargers and this time it's looking to keep Android fans suitably powered up. The Powermat 2X conductive charger with Powercube takes a slightly different tack from previous models of the inductive charging gadget. It has charging tips for specific gadget types, such as Android smartphones.

◀ PROPORTA MIZU II

£15; www.proporta.com

Proporta sells an extensive range of cases and covers for smartphones and tablets of every kind. We like the look of the Mizu II range, with its focus on soft fabrics and muted colours. This particular case fits larger Android phones such as the Google Nexus One.

▶ VISIONEER MOBILITY SCANNER

£199; www.visioneer.com

This 51x70x293mm device is a neat self-contained scanner. It has an SD Card slot and comes with a 1GB memory card to which scanned in items are stored. The scanner can produce colour or black and white PDFs or Jpeg images. ›

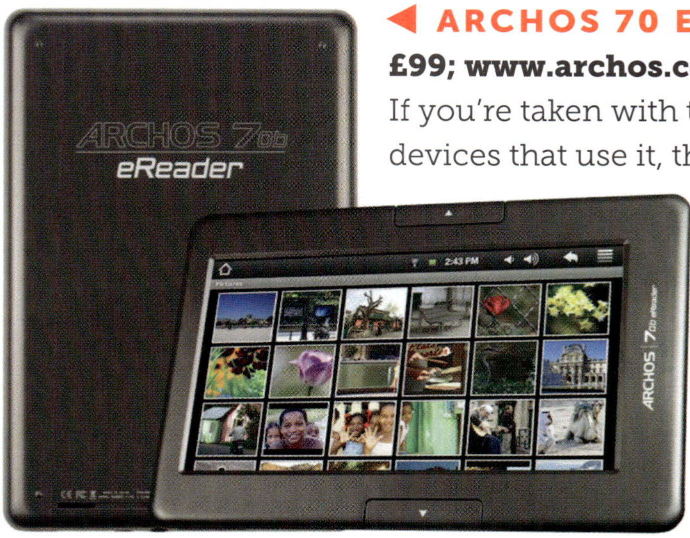

ARCHOS 70 EREADER

£99; www.archos.com

If you're taken with the Android interface and want more devices that use it, the Archos eBook reader could just fit the bill. An alternative to getting a tablet, it has a colour screen, stores hundreds of books on its 4GB internal memory and comes primed with Wi-Fi. The 600MHz processor may not sound that beefy, but since it's serving up only web pages, a few lightweight apps and your eBooks, it ought to be enough.

VOIX GENIE

£39; www.voixltd.com

If you sometimes prefer to use an 'actual' keyboard to type out lengthy memos, the Voix Bluetooth keyboard is worth considering. It sports an attractive tiled keyboard that takes up admirably little space and also doesn't add much heft to an already bulging briefcase: it weighs just 286g. This includes the weight of the built-in rechargeable battery.

BULLGUARD MOBILE

£19; www.bullguard.com

With intelligent gadgets storing more and more of our personal details, it's increasingly important to ensure the information stored on them is kept under lock and key. If your smartphone or tablet ends up in someone else's hands, they have access to almost every aspect of your communications. Security software such as BullGuard can help, even checking for keylogging software embedded in the apps you download from the Android Market and other download sites.

SAMSUNG GALAXY S WI-FI 4.0

£TBC; www.samsung.co.uk

Sticking with the idea of complementary Android devices, comes Samsung's equivalent to the iPod touch. The Galaxy S Wi-Fi player comes in 4in and 5in screen variants and runs Android 2.2. A 3.2Mp camera, Wi-Fi, GPS, Google Maps and support for DNLA media sharing means it's all geared up for beaming music and video over your home.

▶ FREEDOM PRO

£89; www.freedominput.com

We haven't worked out why this is more than twice the price of the Voix Genie, but we guess its down to its diminutive size and its suitability for connecting to a smartphone rather than a tablet. The fold-up keyboard offers a full-size keyboard and dedicated control keys for specific smartphone and tablet functions.

▶ POGOPLUG PRO

£99; www.pogoplug.com

There are plenty of devices that enable you to stream content to or from your Android tablet or phone so you can view your photos or video clips on a large screen TV or a PC monitor. The Pogoplug is the funkiest-looking option we've seen. It allows you to remotely access your files and to view them wherever you like. The device works best over a gigabit Ethernet connection, but also over Wi-Fi and has a free Android app so you can easily get to the items you want.

PROPORTA LEATHER POUCH

£19; www.proporta.com

The Samsung Galaxy Tab is a lovely tablet and we really don't want it to get knocked or scratched. Invest in this leather-look pouch and you'll ensure it's the protective case that looks like it's taken a beating. A clip stops the Tab from sliding out, while inside is a luxuriously soft lining to keep your favourite gadget scratch-free.

▼ CREATIVE ZIISOUND D5

£212; uk.creative.com

The Creative ZiiSound D5 makes it very easy to free up the tunes stored on your Android handset and plays them in crystal clear quality. Since it's Bluetooth, you just need to pair the D5 with whatever smartphone or MP3 player you have.

▼ SEAGATE GOFLEX SLIM

$99; www.seagate.com

The Seagate GoFlex USB hard drive is just 9mm thick and packs in 320GB of hard disk space. It also sports USB 3.0 connectivity and promises backups and file transfers up to 10 faster than with an equivalent USB 2.0 drive.

Get to know Android

Chapter 2

Chapter 2
Get to know Android

This chapter is all about getting started with your new Android device. We look at the operating system's basic features and show you how to give your new handset some personalised tweaks. We also demonstrate how to import existing contacts, use Google Voice to handle texts and voicemail, and how to manage files and documents. >

Android essentials

Get to grips with the basic features of your new smartphone or tablet

Android can do so much for you but, as with any operating system, you have to know where to begin. And it's not just a matter of flicking through the preset features. Compared to the iPhone's set-in-stone interface, Android offers ample room for customisation and control. To whet your appetite, here's a quick round-up of the essentials you should be familiar with.

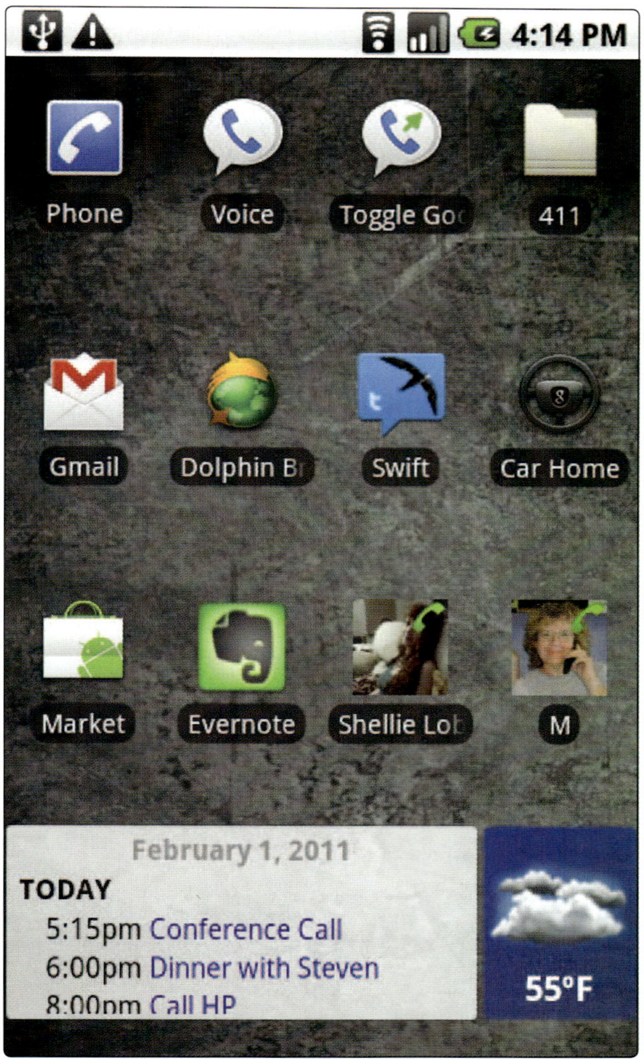

▲ **The Android desktop can be tweaked to show exactly the items you prefer**

THE DESKTOP

The first thing you'll notice about Android is that its desktop differs from those on other smartphone platforms. You have a lot of freedom to make the Android interface your own, and you're not limited to four rows of perfectly aligned square icons. Instead, you can set up your desktop to reflect your interests, and make it as rich and dynamic as you like.

The Android desktop is composed of multiple home-screen panels. Depending on the version of Android that your device uses and on whether it's been supplied with a proprietary 'skin', you may have anything from three to seven panels.

When you power up your phone for the first time, you'll see the main home-screen panel. It's typically centred, so you can access additional panels on either side of this main one by swiping your finger across the screen to the left or right. From Android 2.1 onward, you can also see thumbnail-size icons of all your panels at the bottom of the screen; to jump directly to a panel without swiping, simply tap on the associated icon.

What goes on each of these home screens is up to you. You can fill the space with any combination of shortcuts,

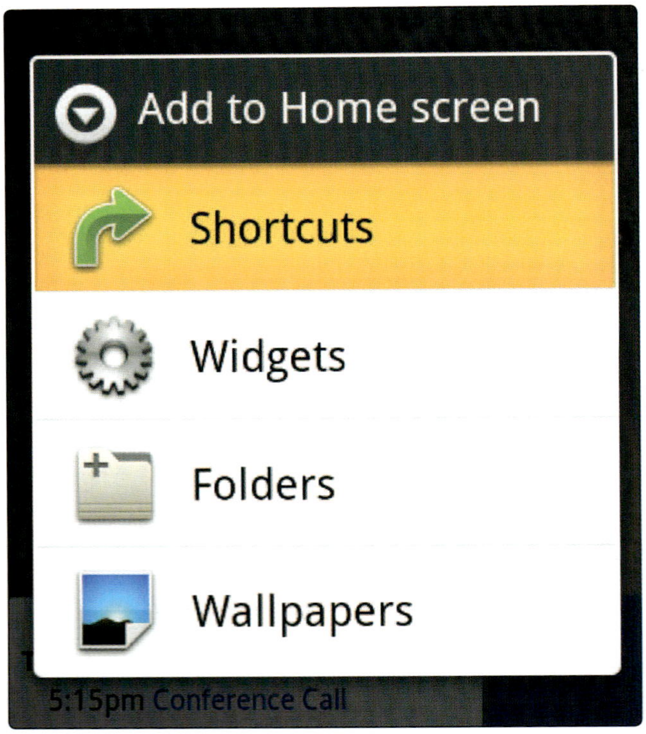

▲ **To add a shortcut, press and hold any empty space, then pick this menu option**

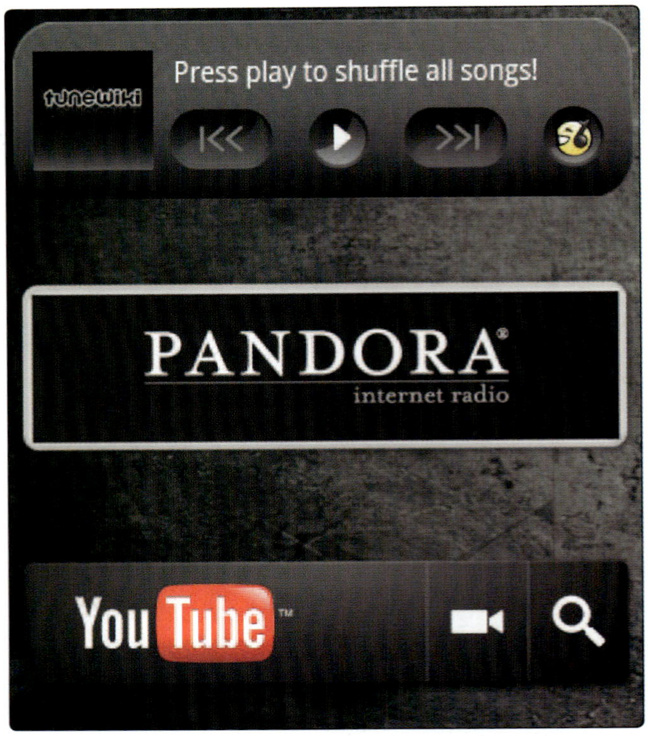

▲ **Android widgets add handy extra features to your device's home screen**

widgets and folders. As you'd expect, shortcuts are small icons that let you load apps or other functions on your phone, and they can do anything from a opening a program to initiating a phone call.

To add a shortcut, just press and hold your finger on any open space on your phone's home screen, and select Shortcuts from the resulting pop-up menu. From there, select Applications to add an app, Direct dial or Direct message to create a shortcut for calling or texting, Bookmark to open a web page or Directions to activate turn-by-turn navigation to a destination in Android 2.0 or higher.

Widgets are dynamic programs that operate directly on your home screen. A widget might, for example, let you play music from your device's memory or from the internet. Limitless options are available from the Android Market.

To add a widget, press and hold on an open space, as above, but this time select the Widgets option from the menu that pops up. Even if you haven't yet downloaded anything from the Android Market, you should have a handful of options built into your device.

Start by adding the Power Control widget, which creates a handy one-touch toggle control for your phone's Wi-Fi, Bluetooth, GPS, data syncing and screen brightness functions.

ORGANISING YOUR ICONS

Folders are a good way to keep your content organised while simultaneously expanding your home-screen space. A ›

folder lets you group multiple shortcuts in a single slot. When you tap on a folder, a box pops up showing all the shortcut icons inside the folder. You could fill one folder with one-touch dialling shortcuts to all of your favourite contacts, and another, perhaps, with various phone-number look-up utilities. Folders help you add many useful things to your home screens without eating up a lot of space.

To add a folder, press and hold your finger on an open space. Select Folders, and then New Folder. Then drag and drop as many shortcuts into the folder as you wish. To give it a custom name, tap the folder once to open it, and then hold your finger along the top bar until the Rename folder dialog box appears on your screen.

To move any shortcut, widget or folder, simply touch and hold your finger to it. After a couple of seconds, it will seem to lift up from the screen. You can then drag it anywhere, including to another panel, and drop it wherever you like. As you drag and drop, you'll also see a trash symbol at the bottom-centre of the screen; slide any icon down on to the trash symbol to remove it from the home screen altogether.

GETTING AROUND

Android phones have four standard keys: a Back button, a Menu button, a Home button and a Search button. These will help you navigate through your phone more easily, no matter what program or process you're running.

The Back key takes you back one step to whatever you were doing before beginning your current step, while the Menu key brings up a list of options relevant to the area of the phone you're currently using. When you press it on the home screen, it permits you to access your phone's settings and other customisation options.

The Home key has two functions. If you press it once, it takes you back to your home screen. If you press and hold it, it allows you to multitask and switch to other programs you've recently used.

Pressing the Search key produces different results depending on where you are in Android at the time. From your

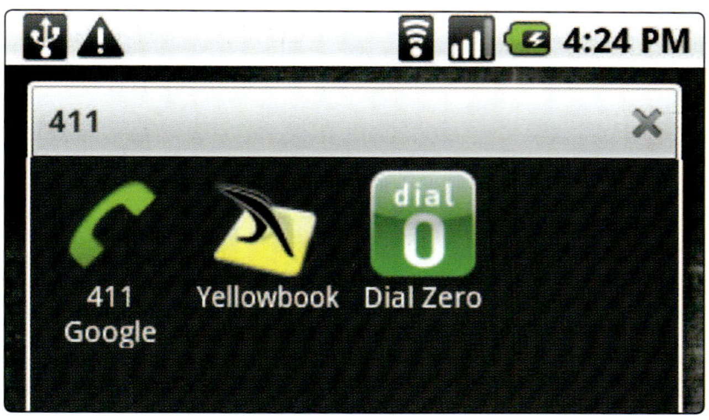

▲ **Folders combine multiple icons into one, saving space on your home screens**

▲ **To delete an icon you don't need, press and hold it and drag it to the Trash**

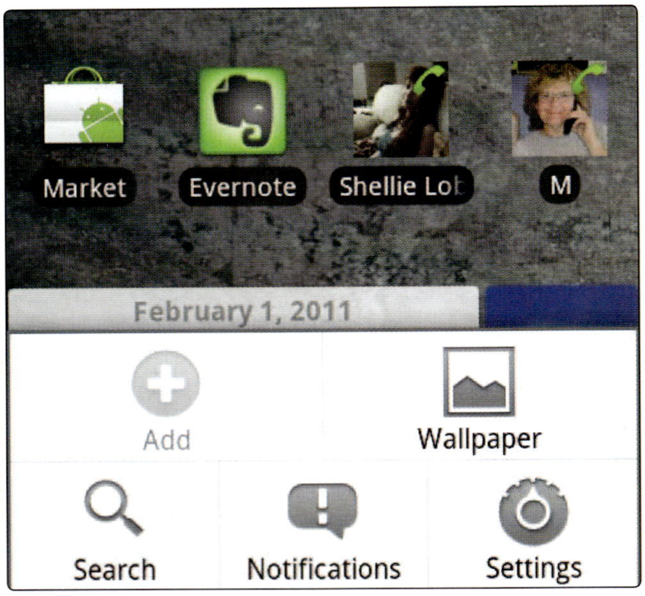

▲ **Tap your device's Menu button to display custom display options**

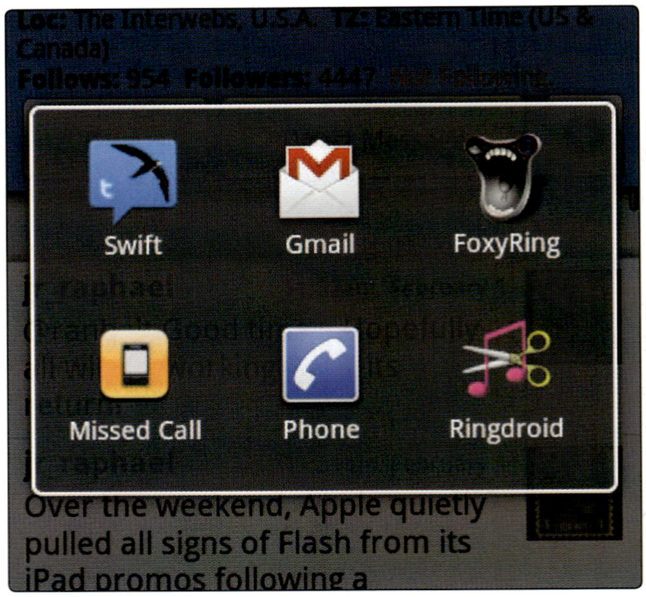

▲ **To launch a link, tap the app you want to use in the selection box that pops up**

device's home screen, it brings up a Quick Search box that you can use to search the web and your phone at the same time (Android will return the most relevant results as you type.)

From within an app, the Search key typically starts a search specific to that app, enabling you to search within your email, for example.

THE APP LAUNCHER

You can always find all your apps in the app launcher. On phones running Android 2.0.1 or earlier, you open the app launcher by touching the grey tab at the bottom centre of the home screen. Starting with Android 2.1 devices, a new square-based icon supplanted the grey tab. The app launcher itself has a slightly different look from 2.1 onwards, too.

Within the app launcher, you can tap any app's icon to run the program, or press and hold it to drag it directly on to your home screen as a shortcut.

NOTIFICATIONS

Complementing Android's ability to deliver 'push' services, which show data as it arrives rather than waiting for you to ask for it, the notification area puts incoming information at your fingertips, no matter what you're doing at the time.

Notifications can come from many different places, such as email, voicemail, or text messages. When you get a new notification, an icon will appear. You can pull down the panel to see detailed information about the notification and then take action if you wish.

Check the settings of the various applications that may be installed on your device to see what kind of notifications they offer, then customise them to work the way you want.

Customise your Android device

Make your hardware truly your own with some personalised tweaks

One of Android's biggest strengths is its flexibility. You can tweak just about every aspect of the interface, from the desktop wallpaper to the blinking LED indicator light. Here's how to give the system a personal touch.

LOOK AND FEEL

The first thing you might want to change is the wallpaper. This couldn't be easier: simply tap the Menu key, then pick Wallpaper. You can select a picture from among your own photos or from the collection of backgrounds supplied. Beginning with Android 2.1, you can also choose any of several 'live wallpapers' that move and even respond to your touch.

Another way to set your wallpaper is directly from the picture gallery. With an image selected, just tap anywhere on the screen and select Set As. You'll be given an option to make the current picture your wallpaper. To extend your options, try using an app such as Backgrounds, a free download from the Android Market. This program gives you thousands of wallpaper designs to choose from and apply directly to your Android desktop.

As we've already seen, the wallpaper is only the beginning: with Android, you can set up your home screens exactly as you like. Another element to play with is widgets. These come in all shapes and sizes; several are pre-loaded, and many others are available either as standalone downloads or as part of fully fledged applications in the Android Market. When you see an app refer to a '1x1 widget', that

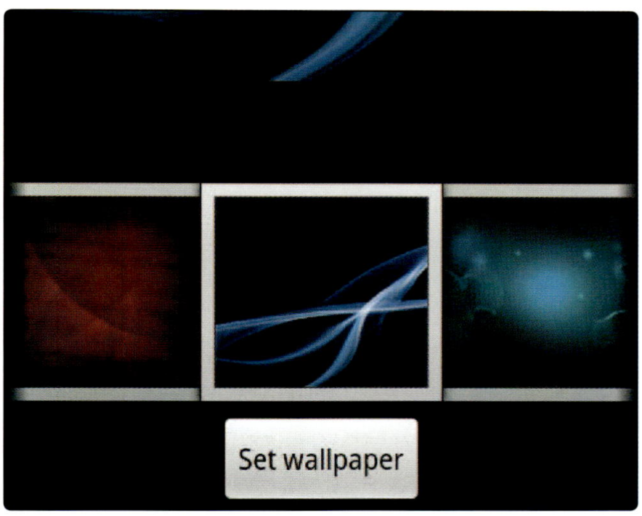

▲ **All Android devices let you customise your handset with your own wallpaper**

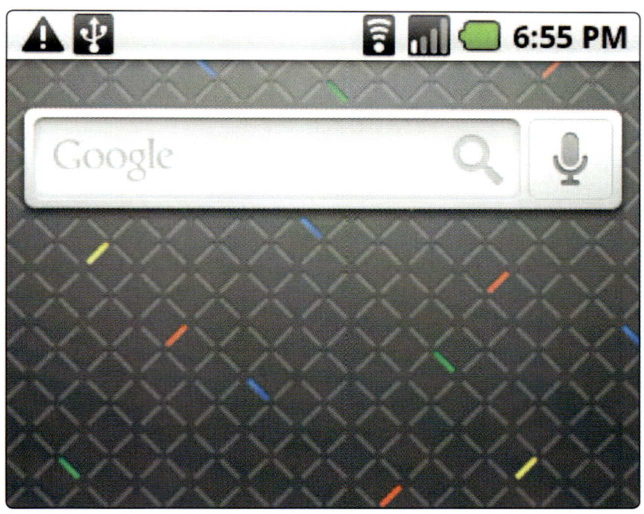

▲ **Since Android 2.1, animated and wallpapers have been supported**

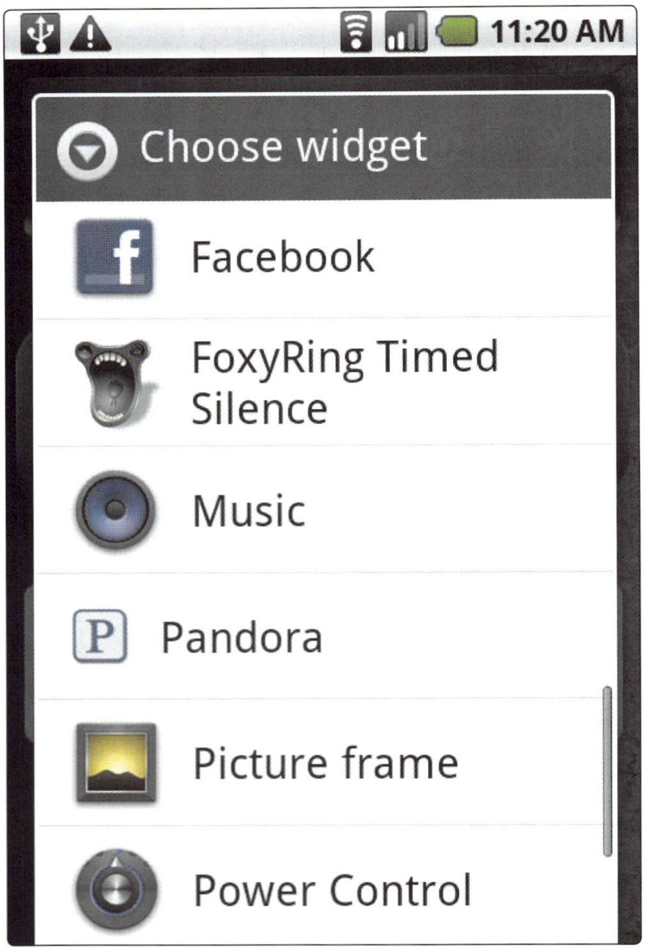

▲ **Widgets for all kinds of purposes are easily added to your home screen**

means the item will take up the space of a single shortcut-size square on your home screen; a 2x1 widget is two squares across and one high, and so on. While some take up entire rows, many useful widgets occupy only one or two squares, helping to make the most of your screen space.

To get you started, check out the free Weather Channel app. This includes a nice 1x1 widget that will detect your current location and keep you up to speed with the latest weather conditions.

For calendar power, try the highly customisable CalWidget, also free. It can put your forthcoming appointments on your home screen in practically any size and colour scheme you could want.

Pandora's free music app includes a 4x1 widget that gives you on-screen controls over playback. The free vizBattery widget puts a 1x1 battery icon on your home screen, so you can always see exactly how much juice you have left.

If you run a blog or website with Google Analytics, take a peek at the Analytics Widget. This shows you your total page views for the day in a 1x1 size.

Remember, each home-screen panel can hold any combination of widgets, shortcuts and folders.

SET YOUR OWN SOUNDS

Itching to make your Android phone's ringtone sound just the way you want? Tap the Menu key and select the Settings menu. From there, tap Sound and Display.

All the basics should now be in front of you, including options to set the default system ringtone, the notification sound, and the volume levels. You'll notice that your own MP3s don't appear in the list of ringtone choices. That's because your phone doesn't yet see them as system sounds. Fortunately, this isn't hard to fix: make a new folder on your memory card called 'ringtones' and copy MP3s into it, and they'll automatically show up in your selection list.

Want to set your own MP3 files as notification sounds or alarms, too? Just repeat the process described above, naming the folders 'alarms' or 'notifications' respectively. If you find ›

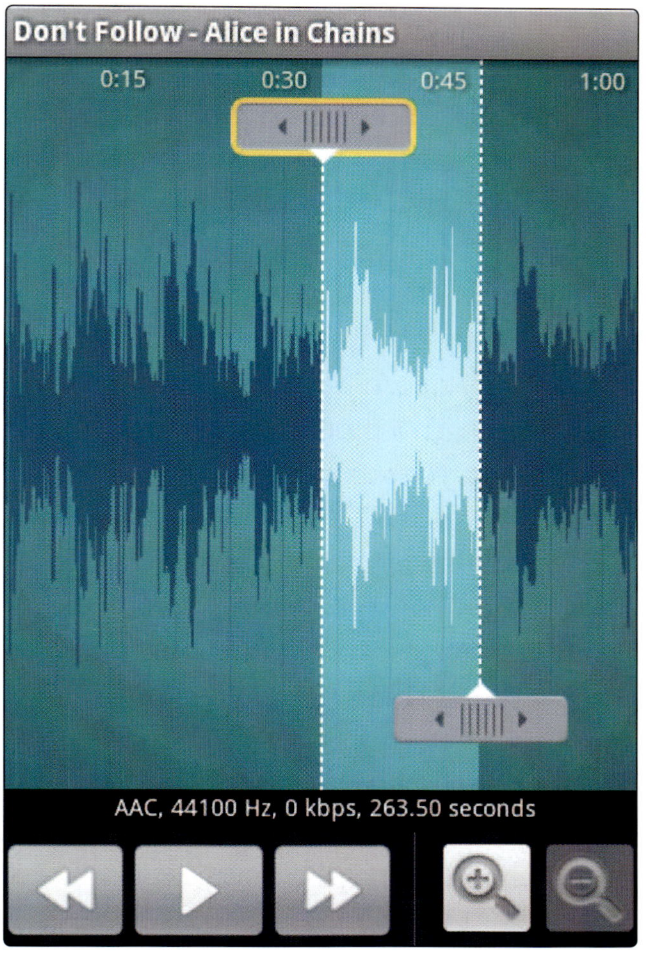

▲ **The RingDroid app lets you cut your desired ringtone out of an audio track**

yourself wanting to use only a certain portion of a song grab the free RingDroid app from the Android Market. With this, it's easy to edit MP3s so that you can get the exact clip you need.

LIGHT ENTERTAINMENT

Most Android devices come with an LED indicator. By default, this usually flashes different colours to alert you to a missed call, or to a new email or text message. But you can make it do much more.

Missed Call, a free app, harnesses the LED to expand your device's notification functionality by making the light flash in specified colours when particular events happen. You could program it to flash orange when you miss a call from your boss and purple when you miss a call from your partner. You can even set flashing LED colours to alert you to calendar items.

MAKE ANDROID DO THE WORK

Personalisation doesn't just mean making your Android device cooler, it can also make your life easier.

Got an annoying colleague who can't take a hint? Route their calls directly to your voicemail and they'll never disturb you again. Just make sure you've entered the offending person's information into your contacts list, then open their profile and press the Menu key. Select Options and select the tick box for Send calls directly to voicemail.

You can control more closely how your phone handles calls and other tasks by installing FoxyRing, free from the Android Market. This app allows you to set custom parameters based on your location. You could have your phone always switch to silent when you're at the local cinema, for example. FoxyRing also allows you to set 'sleeping hours' during which your phone won't ring at all.

For even more robust options, consider two paid-for apps: Setting Profiles and Locale. Available in the Market for £2.50 and £6.25 respectively, these let you set your phone to do all sorts of things based on conditions such as location, day and time or battery status.

The apps can alter everything from advanced sounds to power settings, and even perform complex actions such as opening other programs when preset conditions are met.

NAVIGATE IN STYLE

Depending on your device, using hotkeys to navigate the operating system might save you some time. Android has a built-in set of keyboard shortcuts, but you can create your own. From your home screen, tap the Menu key and select Settings. Next, choose Applications and Quick Launch to set hotkeys for any app.

When it comes to web navigation, you're not stuck with Android's default browser. Third-party alternatives offer powerful extra functionality. Try Dolphin Browser (free from the Android Market, or £3.10 for a licence to remove in-app adverts) for options such as multitouch zooming, gesture-driven control, and seamless link-sharing to social networks.

As for file navigation, you can browse an Android device like a PC using a file manager such as ASTRO, free to download from the Market. This lets you browse through your phone and memory card directories and move files at will.

AUTOCOMPLETE YOURSELF

Finally, a word on Android's autocomplete technology. This can do much more than merely suggest words as you type into the Search box; it can also help you by filling in the phrases you use most often when entering text. The secret is to edit Android's custom dictionary. Tap the Menu key from your home screen and go to Settings, Language and keyboard, then select User dictionary. Try adding your name, your street address, or any phrase you find yourself typing often (for example, 'I'm in a meeting – will call you back when I can'): from now on, those terms will pop up in the autocomplete list as you start typing them.

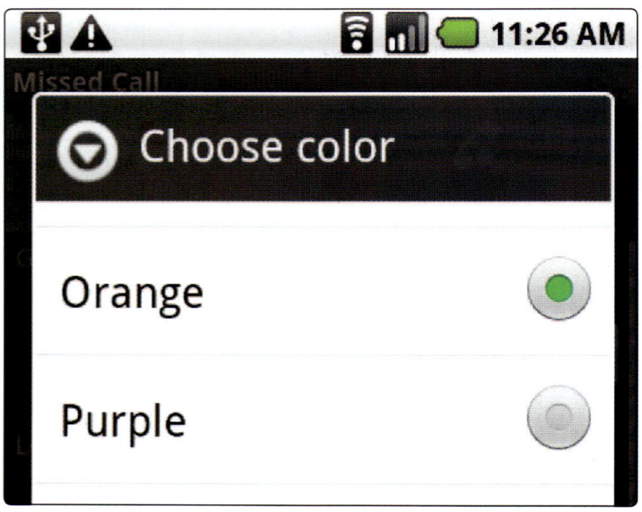

▲ **Apps such as Missed Call use the LED light on your device for notifications**

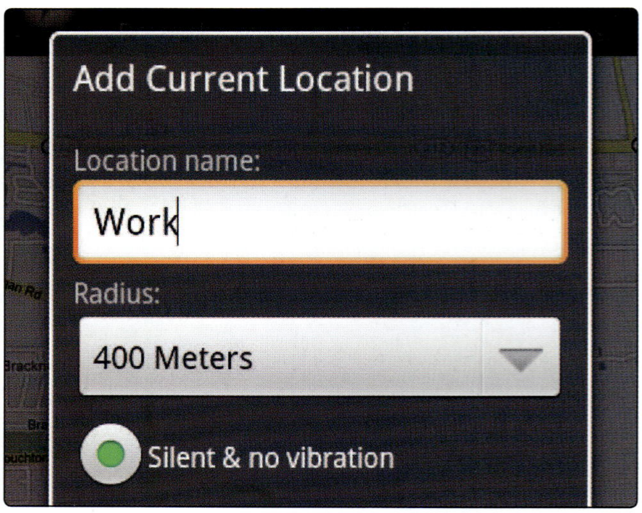

▲ **FoxyRing is a free app that will select ring modes according to your location**

Email and contacts

Bring your existing contacts and email accounts into Android

Google's mobile operating system gives you plenty of ways to stay connected. Here's a tour.

YOU'VE GOT MAIL

Android offers options for both Gmail and non-Google email accounts. When you first power up an Android device, the setup process will help you configure a primary Gmail account, which will automatically appear in the integrated Gmail app, and you'll always see mail appear there instantaneously as it arrives.

In Android 2.0 or higher, you can add other synced Gmail accounts. In the Gmail app, press the Menu key, then select Accounts. Touch the Add account button at the bottom, then follow the prompts. Once the process is complete, you can toggle among your Gmail accounts by pressing the Menu key while in the app and selecting Accounts.

To customise how Android notifies you of incoming messages just tap the Menu key while viewing any account's inbox, and select Settings. If you don't want to be notified of new messages at all, untick the Email notifications box. If you want to receive only a visual notification – an alert in your notification panel and a flashing LED – set the ringtone to silent and untick the Vibrate box.

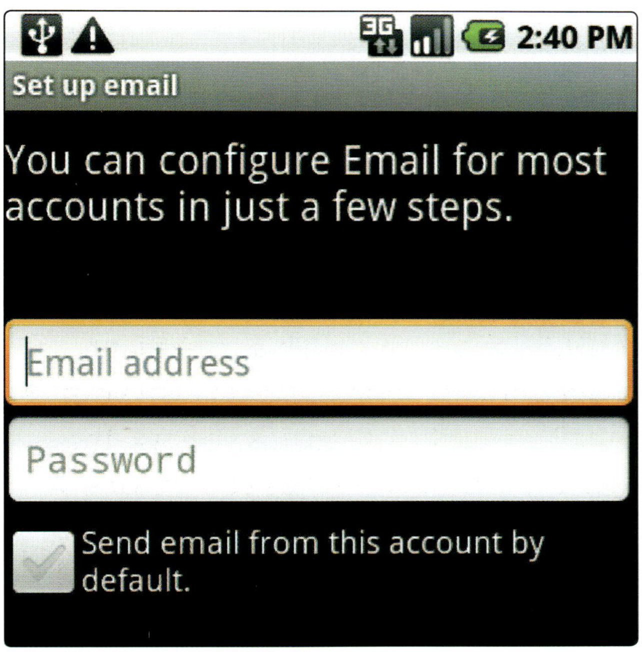

▲ **When you set up your Android device, it'll ask for your Gmail account info**

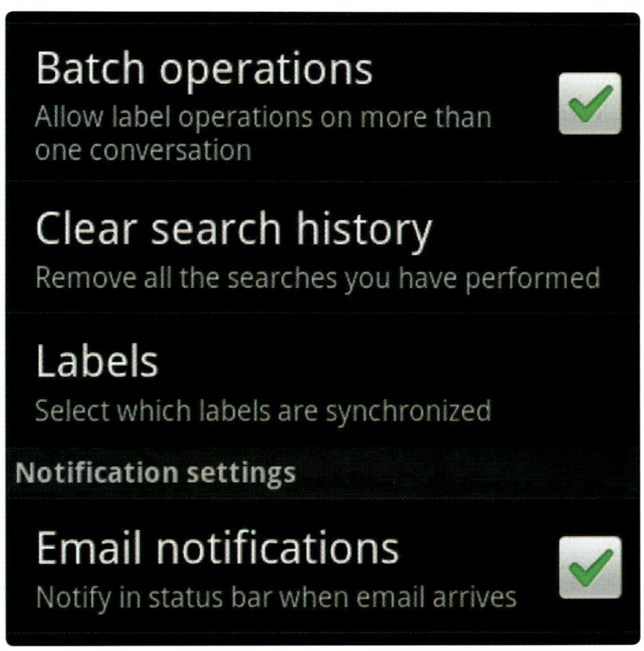

▲ **Tick Email notifications to display an alert with each incoming email**

Social networking and IM

It's easy to keep up with your social networks on your Android device. Facebook, MySpace and Twitter all have official apps to download free from the Android Market, each with a range of notification options. Third-party Twitter apps such as Twidroyd, Swift and Seesmic offer alternative approaches. There's also support for all the major instant messaging (IM) platforms. Google Talk is preloaded on most devices, while apps such as Meebo, free from the Market, let you use this and other IM programs simultaneously, including AIM, Facebook Chat, ICQ, MSN, MySpace and Yahoo.

You can have individual settings for each Gmail account: just repeat these steps from any account's inbox and the changes will apply only to that address.

Any message you'd see in Gmail will now appear in Android too. Your sent, deleted, and even spam messages are also synced by default. Press the Menu key and select the View labels option in Gmail to access all of your different mail folders.

THE COMBINED INBOX

Besides Gmail, Android provides a general email app that can connect to multiple POP, IMAP and Microsoft Exchange accounts. Open the email app (found in the app launcher) and follow the prompts to add any email account you wish.

You have the option of configuring multiple accounts within a combined inbox. While inside the app, tap the Menu key and select Accounts. This lists all the email accounts you've configured. Tap on any account to open it individually, or on Combined Inbox to view messages from all accounts together. You can always add more accounts from this screen, too: tap the Menu key again to find the Add account option.

The email app, unlike Gmail, doesn't support 'push' (except for Hotmail), so messages won't show up instantaneously; instead, the app checks for new mail once every few minutes. You can define how frequently it checks each account in the Account settings menu (press the Menu key while viewing an account).

SYNCING OUTLOOK

Unless you're using an Exchange server, syncing Android with Outlook can be tricky. Google's full Outlook sync utility is available only to paid Google Apps users.

If you're not using Google Apps, try GOGO Contact Sync. This free utility syncs your Outlook contacts with your Gmail contacts. As long as you use the Gmail account you set as your phone's default, contacts will automatically sync from Gmail to your phone. Or try HTC Sync, which we use overleaf.

Install Google's free Calendar Sync utility to sync your Outlook calendar to Gmail, thence to your Android device. >

Step by step: email setup

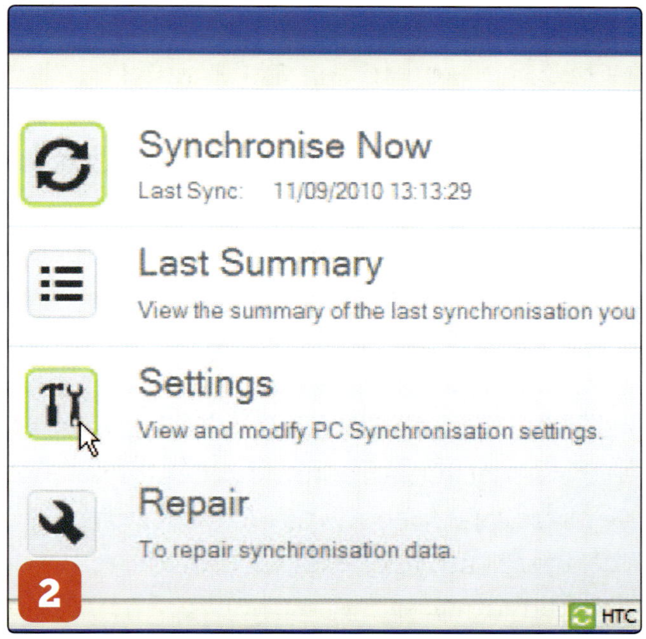

1 Import contacts Your Android device can incorporate contact data from a wide range of sources. On first use it will import your contacts from Gmail. If you also want to add contacts stored on your SIM card, open the Contacts app, press the Menu key and choose Import/Export, then Import from SIM card.

2 Install HTC Sync HTC Sync lets you synchronise the Outlook contact and calendar information on your PC with your phone. Install it from tinyurl.com/2b9sucs and launch the app. Choose Sync Manager, tap Settings, then work through the menu on the left-hand side.

3 Adjust sync settings One setting in particular is very important: it dictates what HTC Sync will do in the tricky situation when the information stored on both your computer and your smartphone has been updated since the last sync. You need to be careful that you choose the correct setting here to ensure that the most up-to-date information is retained following the next sync.

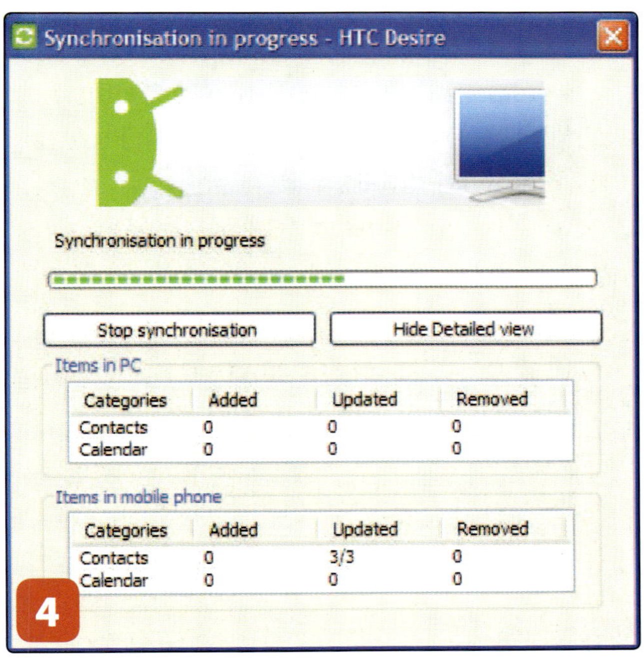

4 Perform sync Having checked that all the settings meet your needs, click Synchronise now. This process can take a little while to complete on the first run, since HTC Sync needs to copy across all the data from PC to phone; subsequent syncs will be faster, with the software looking only for changes made since the most recent sync.

5 Add email You've already configured your device to pick up email from your Gmail account. But it can also cope with other POP and IMAP email addresses. To add a new email account, open the Email app and click Menu, Add Account. Enter your email address and password, then tell Android the type of email account you hold.

6 Enter details Add the required information when prompted. You'll need to know the POP3 and SMTP server information for this email account, which is available from your ISP. Before moving on to each new settings screen, Android will verify the information you have given it and warn you of any errors.

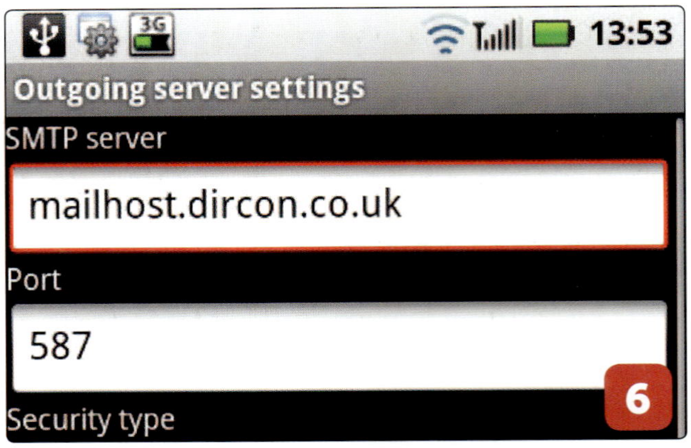

7 Pick options Set the frequency with which the email service should check for new messages and other handset notifications. Also give your account a name. This will be what appears on all of your outgoing mail.

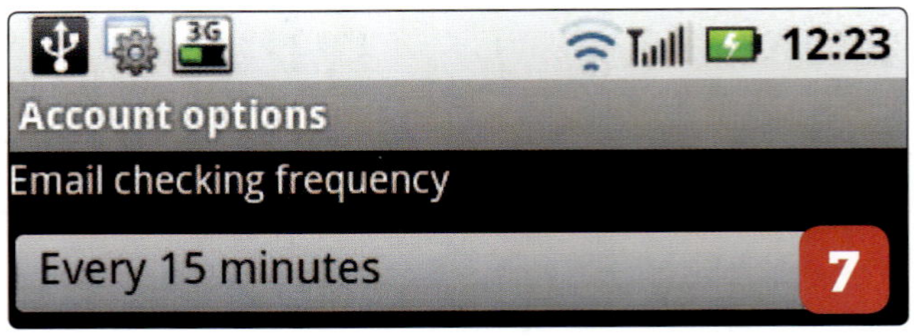

8 Inboxes If you set up more than one email account, you can choose to view mail from each separately or in a single inbox. Press the Email icon, then choose either the combined inbox or select the inbox you want to view.

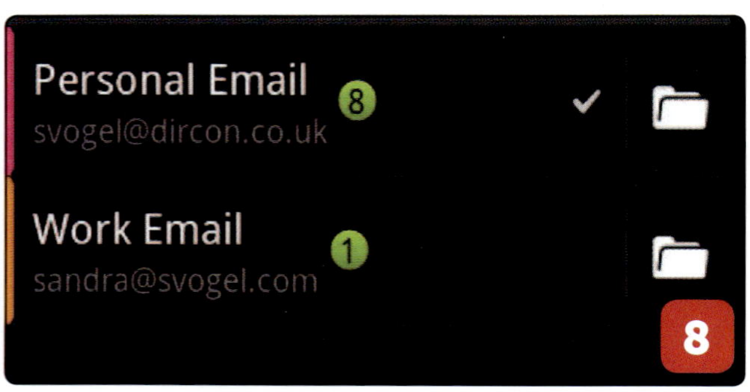

9 Account settings Open any account, hit the Menu button and pick Account Settings. Here you can alter the download frequency. The default account will be used whenever you compose an email.

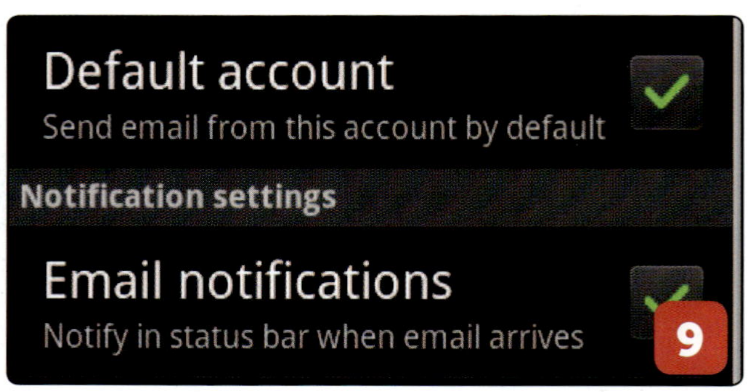

Working with Google Voice

The smart way to handle texts and voicemail on your Android phone

Android smartphones have built-in apps for texting and voicemail, but there's another option: sign up for the free Google Voice service. This provides SMS and voice messaging facilities too, while US and Canadian users can also use it to make cheap phone calls from (and to) a personal number, all over your smartphone's cell connection.

Once you've set up a Google Voice account, open the Google Voice app. This probably came preinstalled on your phone or tablet. (If you can't find it, try the Android Market.) Follow the prompts to connect to your account and you'll be up and running in seconds.

Without getting too far into the nitty-gritty of how Google Voice works, let's take a peek at how you can optimise its features for your Android device. Within the Google Voice app, you can read and listen to any voicemail messages you've received at your Google Voice number, and send and receive text messages for free. Remember, though, that all messages will show as coming from your Google Voice number, not your main mobile phone number.

Originally, Google Voice could only check for new messages at preset intervals of five minutes or more. Now, however, you can opt for near-instant notification by turning on Inbox synchronisation. Open the Google Voice settings on your device and touch Refresh and notification. Select Synchronize Inbox to start receiving faster notifications. This will automatically disable the option to forward texts to

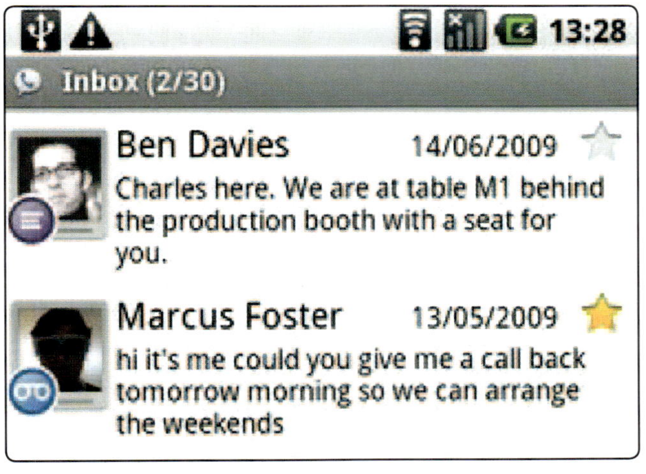

▲ **One benefit of texting via Google Voice is that messages are completely free**

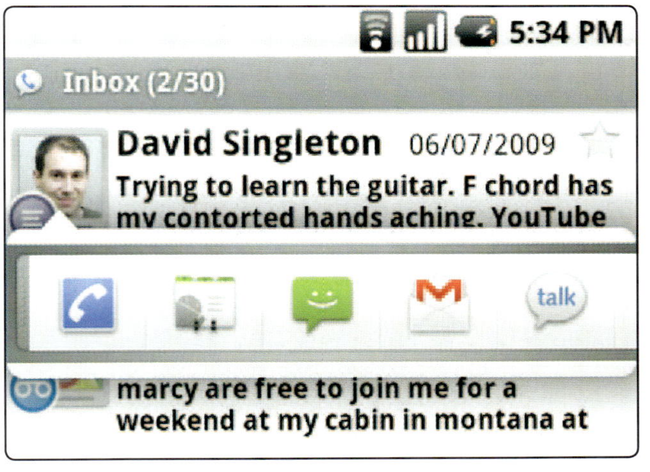

▲ **Click on any photo to get options to respond to their voicemail by email**

Extending Google's Voice

There are a number of different options on the Android Market if you wish to extend Android's voice-recognition capabilities, although not all speech-recognition engines were created equal.

Edwin, Speech-to-Speech (free), for example, listens to you, and recognises what you're saying. Unusually, it then talks back. At its best Edwin feels like talking to a person – not the most creative person you'll ever meet, but a person nonetheless.

Or you could pack up your Android device and go multilingual. **Talk To Me Classic** (also free) offers translation from and to up to seven languages – outputting the results as SMS (text) or email (text and voice) – so long as you own the language. Sample language packs come for free, but most are paid for. Where there's not a language pack, you can still see the translation but not send them on.

your mobile number, so you won't get the same messages twice.

Alternatively, you might want to route your messages via Gmail. Log in to the Google Voice website from a PC. Click Settings and choose Voicemail & SMS. Under Voicemail Notifications, tick the options to email both voicemail notifications and SMS messages to your Gmail account. From now on, every time you receive a voicemail or text message via Google Voice, you'll get an email notification to Gmail, which will pop up instantaneously on your Android device. You can even reply to a text message by responding to the email; Google will automatically route your response to the sender's number as a regular SMS.

If you go this way, you may want to disable notifications within the Google Voice app, as they'll be redundant. To do this, again, tap the Menu key while in the Google Voice app and select Settings, then touch Refresh and notification and adjust the options as you prefer.

Finally, if you go back and forth between using your Google Voice number and your mobile phone number for calls, add the Toggle Google Voice shortcut to your home screen. (Under the main Shortcuts menu; tap and hold your finger on any open space on your home screen, then select Shortcuts to find and add it.) This gives you a one-tap switch to change which number you're using to dial out.

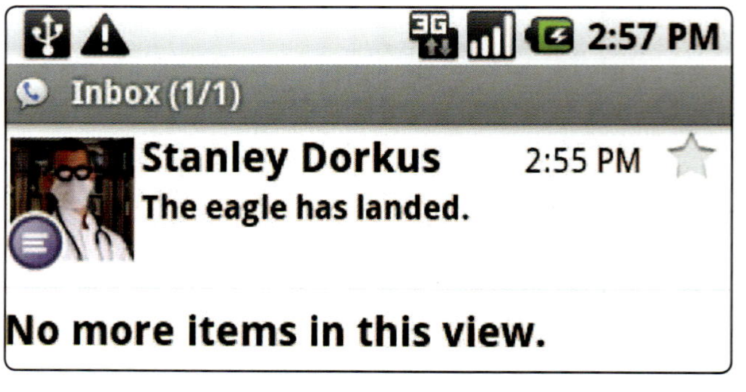

Google Voice transcribes your voicemails into text as well as playing the audio

Managing files and documents

Android doesn't come with a file browser or editor, but help is at hand

All play and no work makes your smartphone an expensive toy. But with the help of a wide selection of professional-grade mobile apps from the Android Market, your Android device can get down to business. Here's an overview of some of the best apps for viewing, creating and editing business documents on the go.

FILE MANAGEMENT

You have several ways to move files onto, off and around your Android phone. The easiest method is to connect your device to your PC with a USB cable and mount it as a drive: tap the Android notification area, select USB Connected and tap Mount. You can then click through your SD card's contents, explore and create folders, drag files around, or copy items between the device and your PC's hard disk, just as you would to any PC storage. This is a simple way to get your most important files on to your handset so that you can carry them everywhere you go.

Of course, if you always had your PC handy, you probably wouldn't need to carry files on your phone in the first place. So you'll want a reliable tool to help you explore the files and folders on your phone when your computer is nowhere in sight. One of our favourites is ASTRO

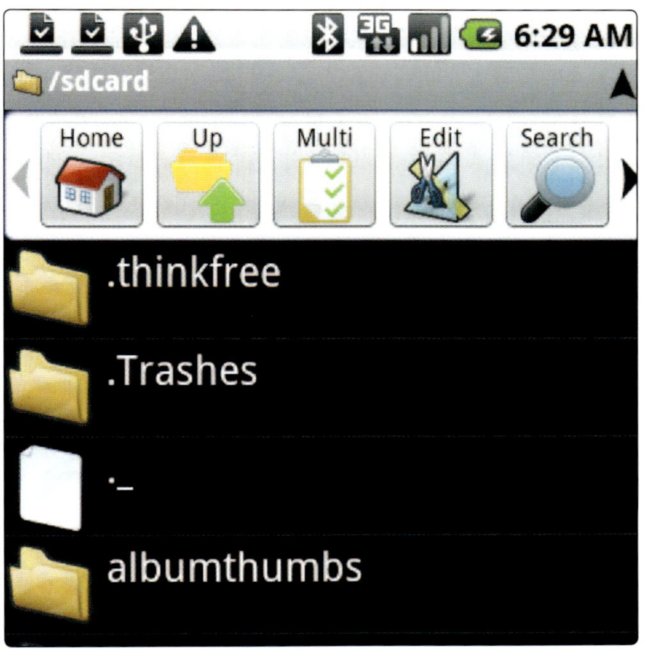

▲ ASTRO File Manager makes it easy to navigate the contents of your device

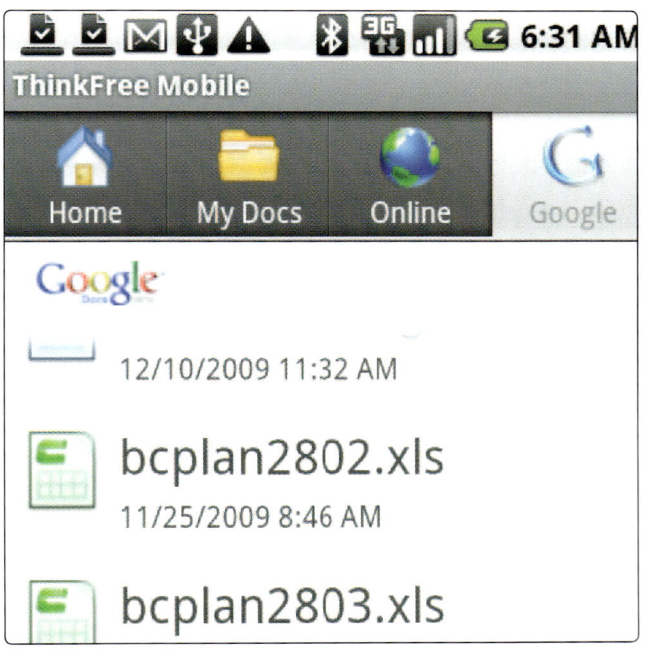

▲ ThinkFree Mobile connects to Google Apps to let you view your documents

File Manager. Free from the Market (or £2.45 for an ad-free version), it gives you a Windows-style view of all your folders, files and documents. Whether it's a word-processor document, a photo or a music file, you can get quick previews of a file's contents or tap the item to open it. Android will prompt you to choose which application to open it with; you'll also have the option to set your choice as the default option for future instances.

In ASTRO's menu bar are options to move, copy, rename or delete files. Tap the Multi option and you can select multiple files or folders to work with at once. In addition to working with files and folders, ASTRO File Manager can back up installed apps and browser bookmarks and kill unwanted processes that could otherwise drain your battery.

ThinkFree Mobile Office works in a similar way, and for £9.63 you can upgrade it to a full suite of viewing apps for all kinds of documents. The premium version enables all the features in ThinkFree Write, ThinkFree Calc and ThinkFree Show, which handle text, spreadsheets and presentations respectively and can display Microsoft Office files with most of their original formatting. ThinkFree also connects to Google Docs to download and view files saved in the cloud.

Though advanced editing features generally come only with paid apps, a free utility called GDocs lets you view, edit and even create basic documents in Android. Rather than do all the dirty work on your device, it connects to Google Docs, storing your documents in Google's cloud-based applications. GDocs itself creates only text files, and launches a web browser to view spreadsheets and presentation documents in Google Docs.

▲ **Documents To Go is the next best thing to a complete office suite for Android**

If you need to do more work on your phone, DataViz Documents To Go is even more robust and reliable for business users on Android than on BlackBerry and other mobile platforms. This £9.21 app suite (there's also a view-only free version) lets you view and edit existing Office documents and create new documents in Android. It can even edit charts, a feature that's well beyond the capabilities of most mobile business apps. >

Step by step: file management

1 Install a file manager Android doesn't come with the type of file manager you're accustomed to on your PC, so you'll miss the ability to browse documents, move around or delete media stored on your memory card and organise email attachments. Fortunately, there are plenty of third-party file manager applications you can add. We like OI File Manager, a free download from the Android Market.

2 Browse your memory Once installed and launched, the application can browse the contents of your handset and any media cards being used. If you can see a Home icon at the top of the folder list and an SD Card icon beneath it, you're currently looking at the device memory. Tap the SD Card icon to browse the contents of your media card, and the Home icon to return to the phone's internal memory.

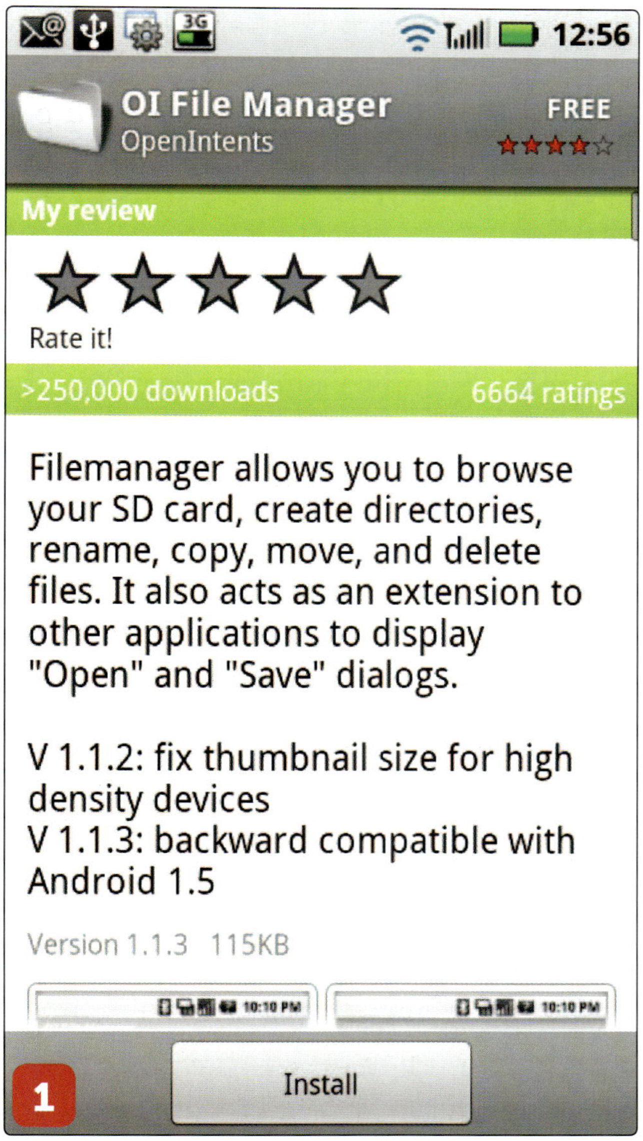

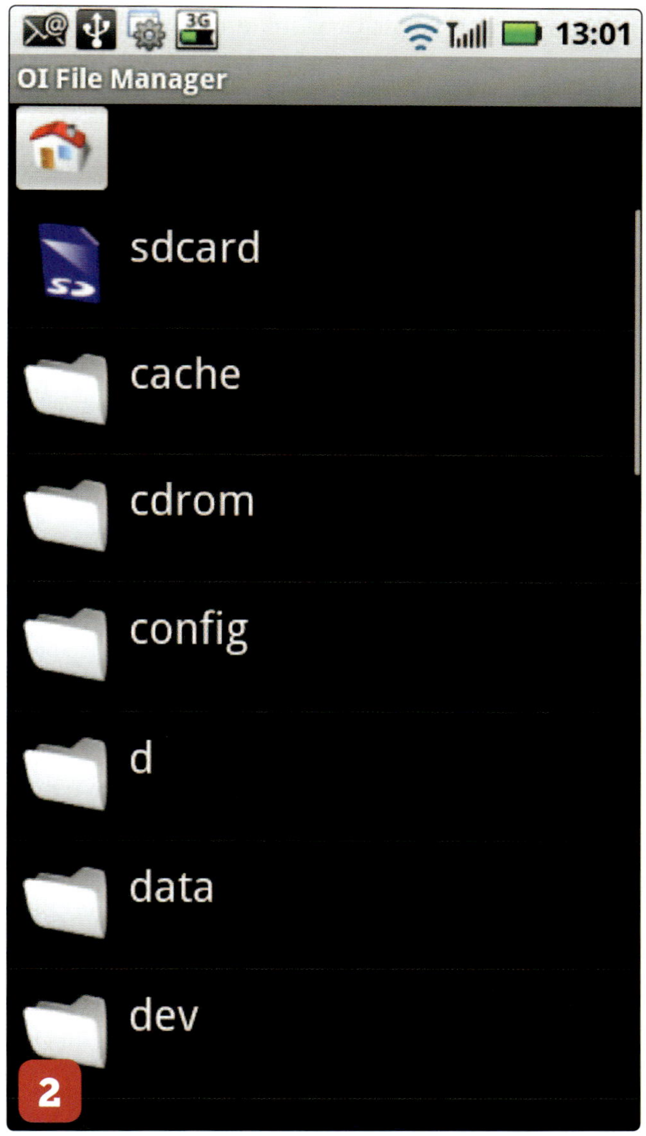

3 Create a folder OI File Manager also lets you create new folders (or rename existing ones), then move files into them. To create a new folder on the media card, tap the SD Card icon, then tap the Menu button and choose New Folder. Give it a name.

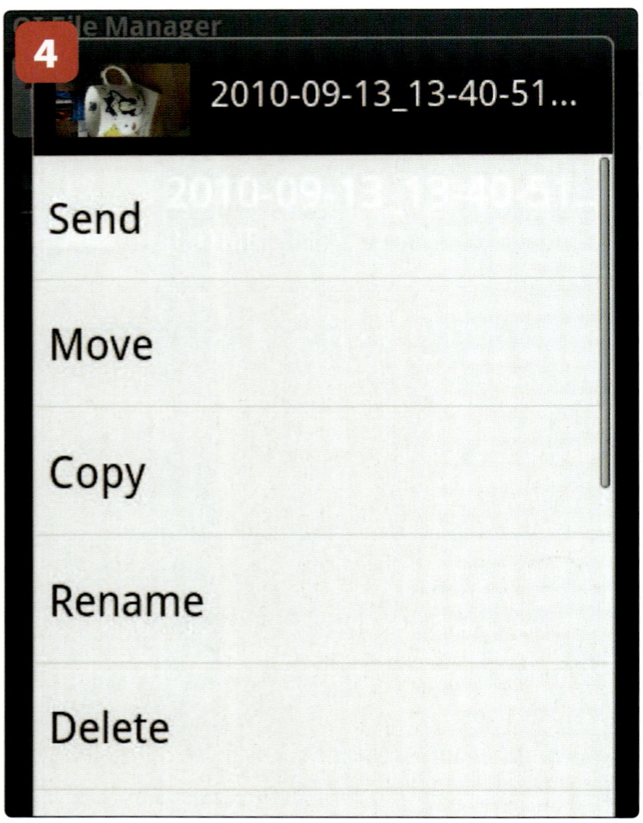

4 Organise files To copy, move, rename or delete a file, you need only find it and then hold a finger down on it. You'll see different options depending on the file type. Choose Send to transfer the file to another device using Bluetooth or email.

5 Rename files Mobile devices have a tendency to generate files with meaningless names, such as photos your camera labels with sequential numbers. One of the benefits of a file manager app is that you can easily rename important files. The only caveat is that you must be careful not to edit the file extension (the three letters after the dot), or the file may become unreadable until the correct extension is put back. Hold a finger down on a file and choose Rename, and a box will appear in which you can enter a new name.

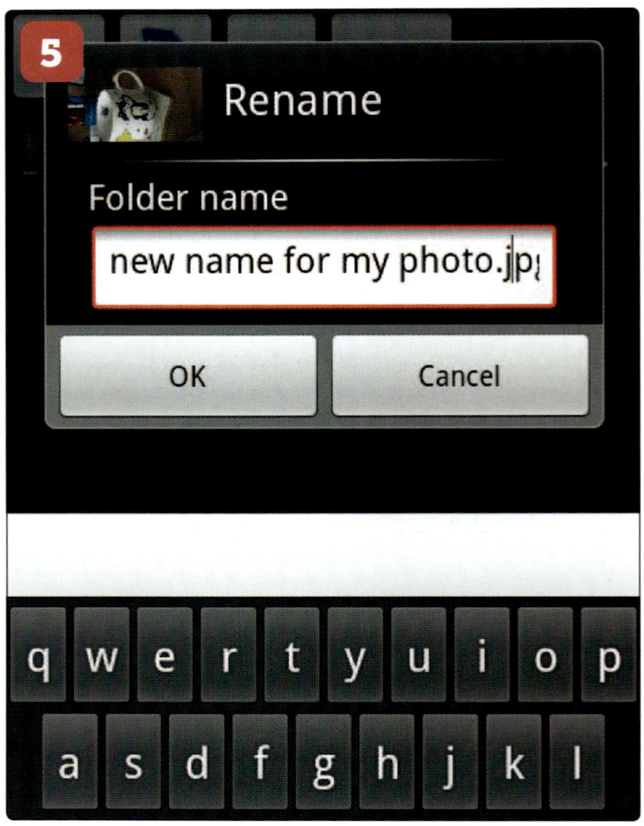

subscription.co.uk/pcadvisor/andr

>> pcadvisor.co.uk/news >> twitter.com/pcadvisor >> facebook.com/pcadvisor
>> mobile.pcadvisor.co.uk >> tinyurl.com/PCALinkedIn

STRAIGHT TO YOUR DOOR • BE THE FIRST TO READ PC ADVISOR

Letter from the Editor

PC Advisor hit the news stand in 1995. Not every family had a PC, and if they did it was a noisy beige box used for spreadsheets, newsletters and the occasional game. Surfing the net mostly meant using dial-up: snarling up the phone line to find atrocious-looking websites. Such days are gone.

> "There's no better way to get expert advice"

In the past 16 years, we've covered the inexorable rise of the internet, an exponential increase in computing performance, and the birth of the mobile- and cloud-computing eras.

Along the way we've seen false starts and spats, technology successes and failures, and malware that refused to die. We've watched as Microsoft slowly got to grips with PC security, Google swallowed the world whole, and Apple defied those who believe that substance always beats style (it doesn't).

Join us

Now we can all access everything, at any time, from everywhere, PC Advisor is bigger and better than ever. Our unrivalled team of experts continues to bring you news of the latest PC hardware and software, as well as independent, lab-tested reviews of the world's best technology products.

Each month we review hundreds of computer products, cover thousands of news stories, and write yet more features and expert guides. And to the latest issue of the magazine we bring only the most interesting and important of each.

If you're an expert in computing, an interested hobbyist, or a total beginner, there's no better way to get expert advice you can trust than with a subscription to PC Advisor. Join the PC Advisor team and enjoy the next 16 years of computing in the best company possible.

Matt Egan, Editor, PC Advisor
matt_egan@pcadvisor.co.uk

facebook.com/pcadvisor

twitter.com/pcadvisor

tinyurl.com/PCALinkedIn

IDG After three issues for £3, your PCA subscription will continue at the discounted rate of £39.99 for 12 issues or £19.99 for six issues. You'll receive 12 issues in a 12-month subscription. We will also give you a full refund on any unmailed issues if you ever decide to cancel. Your subscription will start with the next available issue. For overseas rates please call +44 1858 438 867 and quote ANDR.

Music, video and photos
Chapter 3

Chapter 3

Music, video and photos

These days your smartphone is much more than simply a tool for calling friends and family. It's a multimedia device that's perfect for listening to your favourite tunes or catching up on the latest TV. And with most models coming with integrated cameras, it's now easy to take pictures or shoot video, and then share them. In this chapter, we look at how to make the most of Android's built-in multimedia features.

Playing music

Your Android device is ideal for listening while you work or play

Android is a great platform for mobile communications, but it's also designed from the ground up to offer a rich multimedia experience. Your Android device is jam-packed with features that let you manage and play your digital music in a variety of ways.

Like Apple's iPhone, Android has a built-in music player with a touchscreen interface that's easy to use while you're on the go. Because Android is an open platform, you'll find no shortage of third-party apps that go well beyond the capabilities of the basic app. We look at some of these in Chapter 5.

Here we'll explore Android's music management features and see how you can get music onto your device from a computer or directly from Amazon.

LOADING YOUR TUNES

Some device vendors have come out with customised desktop applications to help PC users manage media on their Android devices. These programs are sometimes useful, but not essential for copying music and other files from your computer to your phone. All you need to do is connect the device to your PC's USB port and touch the notification area at the top of your device's screen. Tap 'USB connected' in the notification area, then tap Mount to make your phone or tablet's memory appear as a storage device on your desktop. This works the same way in Windows, Mac and Linux.

Once your computer mounts the Android device's storage, you can open it to view the files and folders on your device. Simply locate any DRM-free music

▲ Connect to a USB port and tap Mount to make your Android device's memory visible on your PC as a storage device

files on your computer's hard drive (or any connected drive where you store your media, such as a NAS box) and drag them to the Music folder in Android.

WINDOWS MEDIA PLAYER

Most Android devices don't come with their own desktop sync utilities. But if you want the convenience of automatic synchronisation in Windows, you already have a desktop application for the job: Windows Media Player.

To sync your music tracks (as well as your pictures and videos) with Media Player, first follow the same steps as above. Plug your Android phone or tablet into your PC's USB port, tap USB connected in Android's notification area, and tap Mount to make your PC recognise it as a storage device.

Then launch Windows Media Player and wait for your phone to appear as a drive letter in the left pane of Media Player's Library view. To set up syncing, click the Sync tab in the upper right corner of Windows Media Player and then click the small (and unlabelled) Sync options drop-down menu under that. Click Set up sync... and then either name your device or leave it as the drive letter, as you prefer. When you click Finish, you'll have a sync relationship configured so that your phone will update to mirror your PC's Music folder whenever the device is connected via USB.

THE AMAZON MP3 STORE

As well as transferring music from your PC to your phone via USB, you can buy songs and albums from Amazon's music store and download them directly to your Android phone or tablet over the air, without having to use a computer or a USB connection.

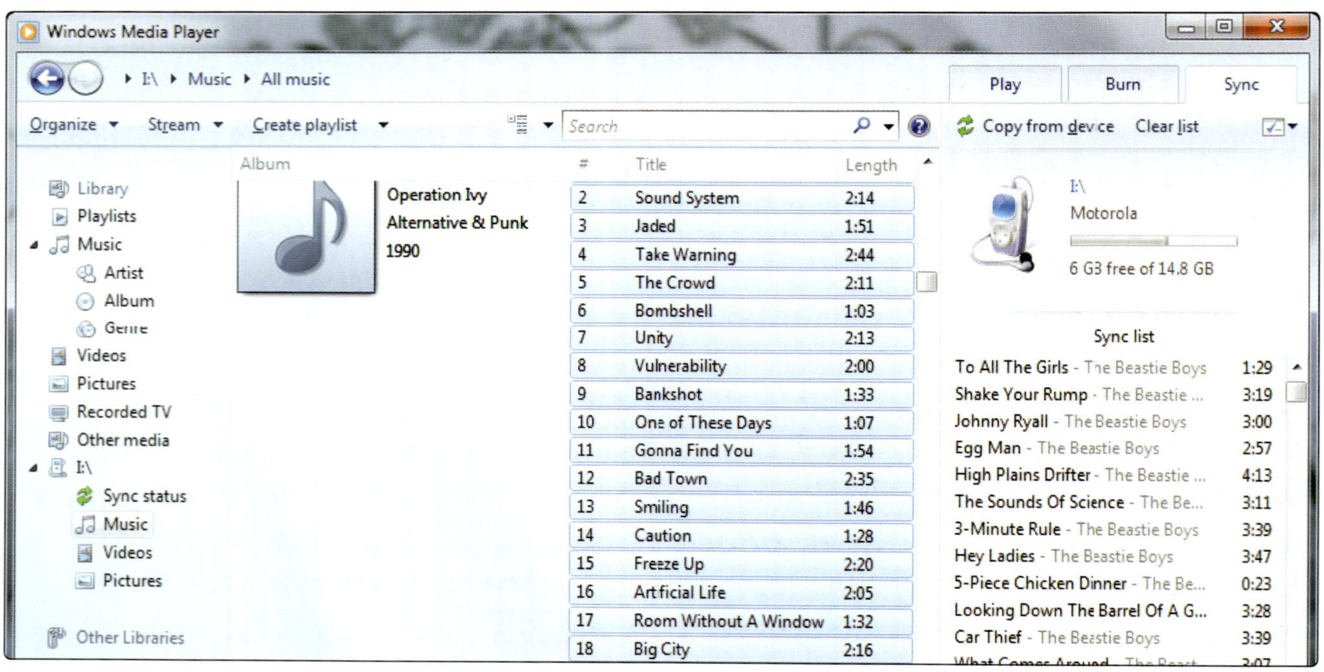

▲ **Windows Media Player makes a good desktop client for your Android music library**

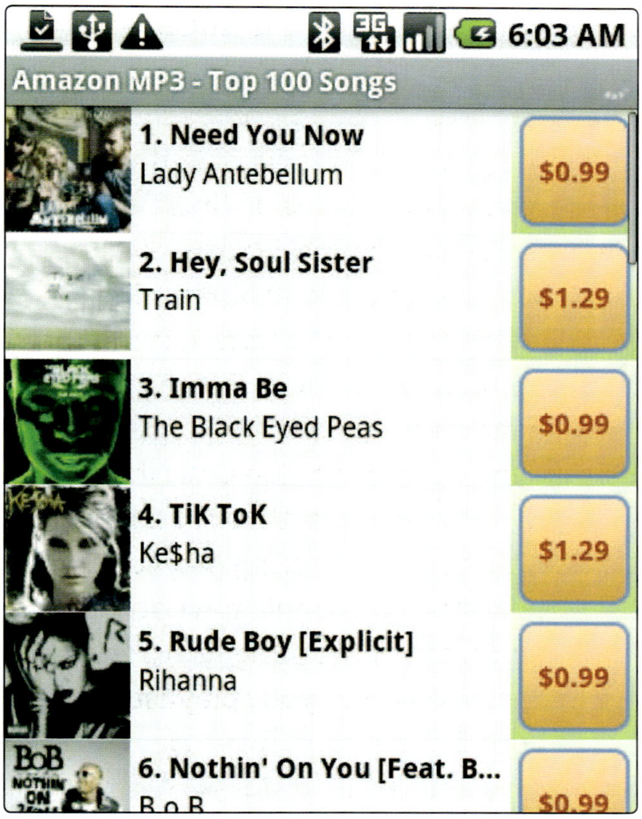

▲ **Tap the price button to buy any song in Amazon's store. You can then transfer it to your Android device via 3G or Wi-Fi**

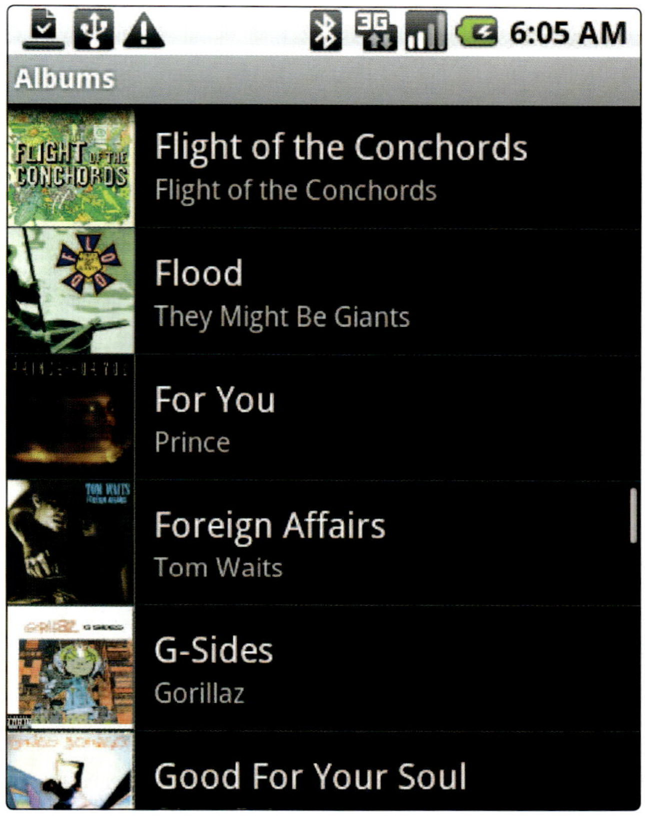

▲ **In your Albums list, thumbnails of the album artwork make it easy to find the music you're looking for at a glance**

Tap the Amazon MP3 icon to enter the store, where you'll be greeted by options to view the top 100 albums, see the top 100 tracks, browse by musical genre, or search for tunes. To hear a 30-second preview of any song, tap its title. When you find a song or album you want, tap its price button once; the word 'Buy' will appear. Tap it again, and you'll see an Amazon login screen. Enter your Amazon-registered email address and password to continue. If you'd like to speed through this process next time, tick the box to enable 1-Click ordering.

Once you've completed the purchase process, the song (or songs) will begin downloading. You may be prompted to switch to a Wi-Fi connection; this isn't obligatory for downloading music (as opposed to video), but if you have access to a Wi-Fi network it's generally the fastest way to get songs onto your device.

When downloaded, your Amazon music downloads live in a folder labelled 'amazonmp3' on your device's memory card. As a precaution against data loss, you can connect your device to a PC and drag your purchased songs over to its hard drive to save them as a backup. Since the songs are sold DRM-free, you can then also listen to them on your computer if you want to.

THE MUSIC APP

When you tap the blue speaker icon for Google's built-in Music app, you'll find yourself at the app's very simple home screen, which is divided into four options that let you search your music collection by artist, album, song title or playlist. Tapping any of these four items will take you into an alphabetised list that you can scroll through to select the music you want to hear. Also available from the home screen are two menu options that you can access by pressing the Menu button on your phone. The first, Party Shuffle, will instantly create a randomised playlist of everything in your music library. The second, Search, lets you track down any album or track by name.

To create playlists on your phone, tap and hold any song title until the context menu appears, then tap Add to playlist. Choose an existing playlist or tap New to create and name a new one. You can then return to the song list to select more tracks to add to your playlist.

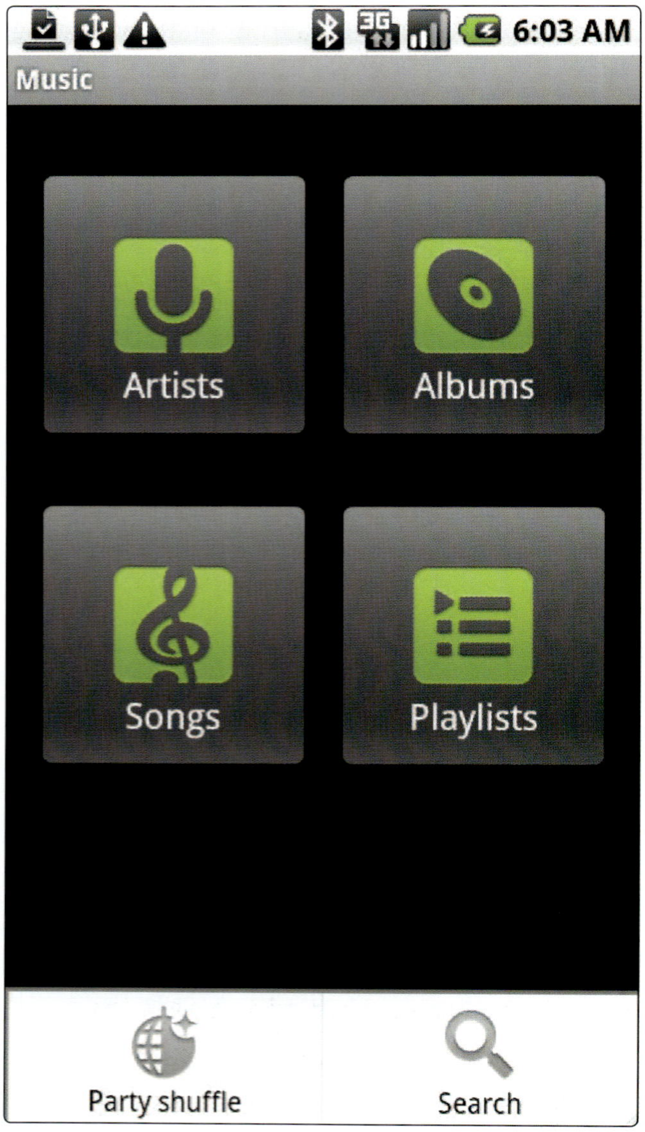

▲ **Android's Music app makes it easy to navigate through your tunes. Note the Party shuffle and Search options**

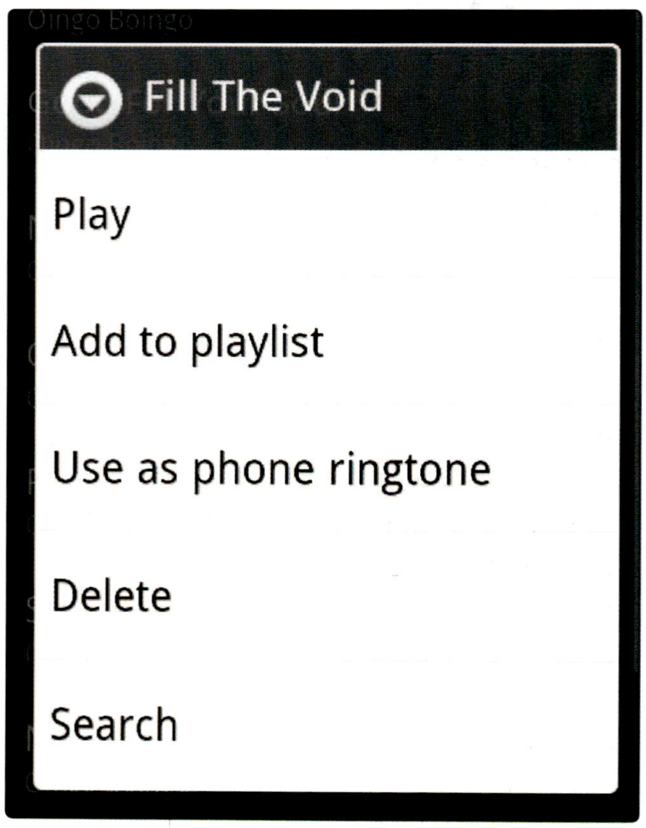

▲ **Playlists help organise your listening. To add any song to a playlist, tap and hold it, then choose Add to playlist**

Accessing iTunes

Play your iTunes library on Android with doubleTwist

BlackBerry owners have support for iTunes built in, but users of other mobile platforms aren't so lucky. For Android handsets, doubleTwist is a mobile app that lets you access anything in your iTunes library for playback on your phone. Download it from doubletwist.com and allow it to access the Registry.

1 Launch doubleTwist You'll be offered an upgrade to the paid-for AirSync version. We're going to use the free USB synchronisation instead. Plug in your handset and enable mass storage device access if required. You may need to prompt Windows to find your phone by clicking the 'start a network scan' option.

2 Style icons Use the Pictures, Videos and Music icons in the left panel to see what doubleTwist has located on your hard drive. It has a number of 'watch' folders for your user profile, music library and shared music, for example. You can also specify iTunes playlists to import by selecting this option from the Library drop-down menu.

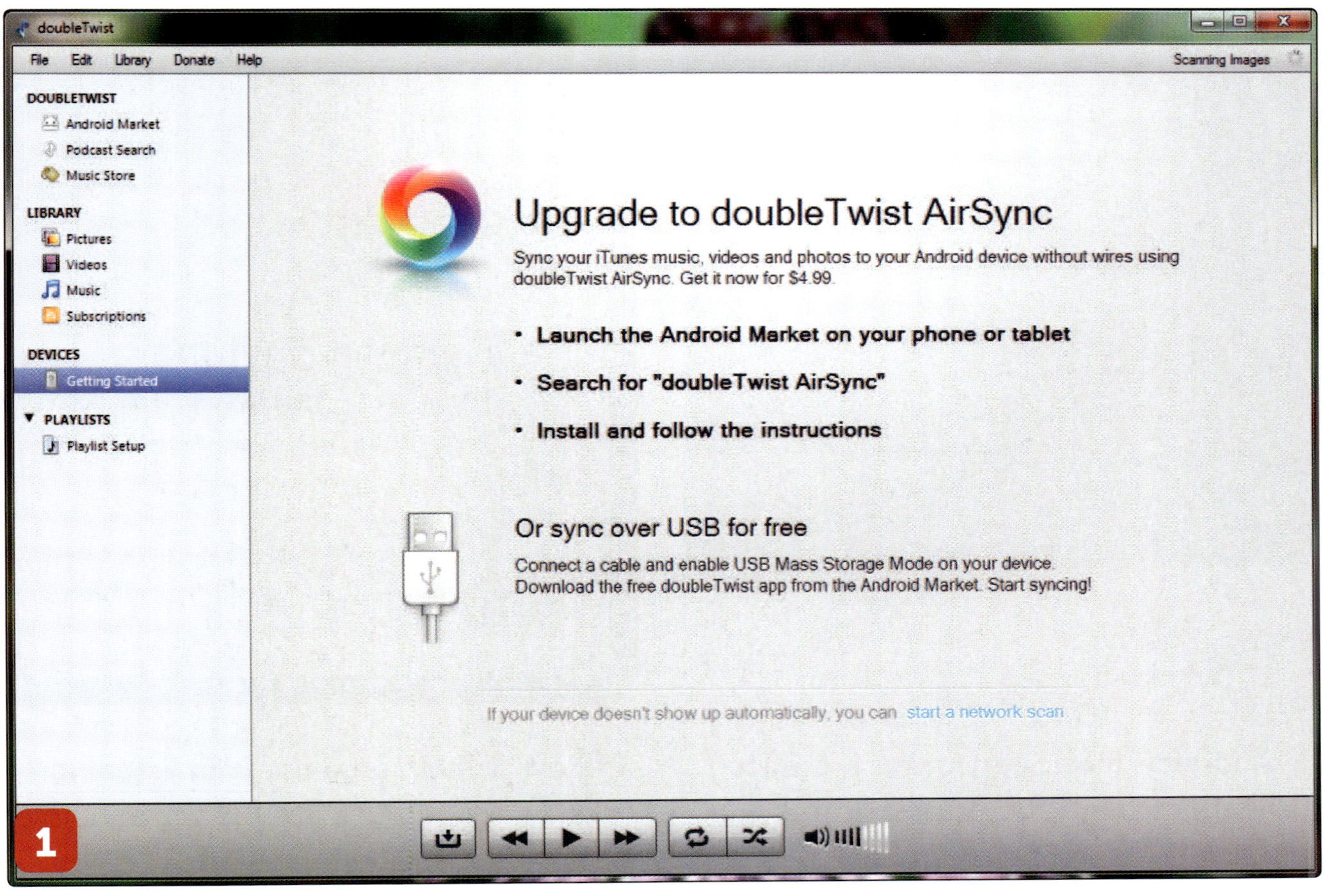

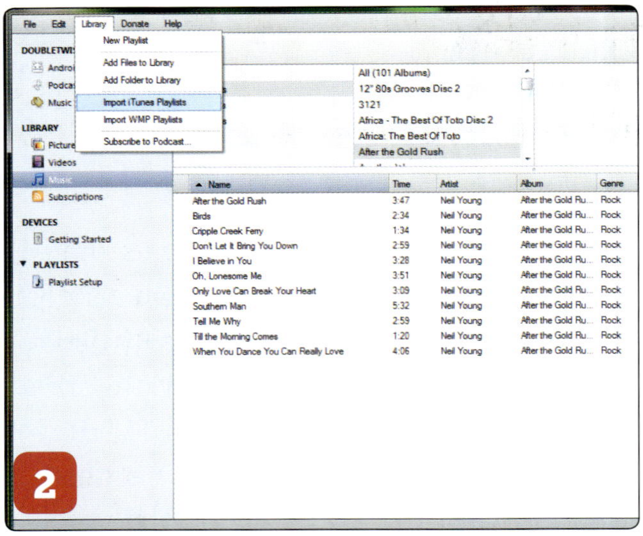

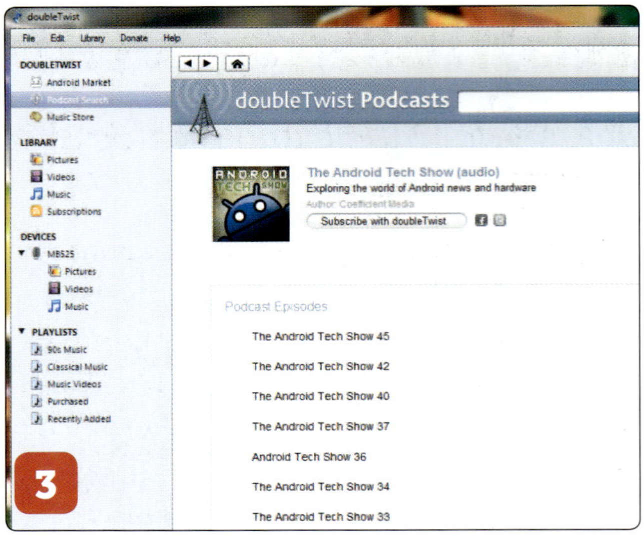

3 **Choose your content**

You can now choose which items and types of content you want to synchronise between your PC and smartphone. doubleTwist shows you how much space you have available on your Android phone or tablet, and lets you add more details about the device. Music and podcast subscriptions can also be synchronised.

4 **Adjust settings**

The easiest option is to synchronise all your music. However, for storage space reasons – or simply because you don't often listen to some artists – you may prefer to select specific albums. The photo tab allows you the option of automatically copying items from your handset to its PC-based library for backup.

5 **Sync your music**

Press the Sync button when you're ready to start copying files. You will need to perform the full synchronisation only once, but your Android device must remain connected to the computer until the process is complete. Future syncs can be limited to 'Recently added' files.

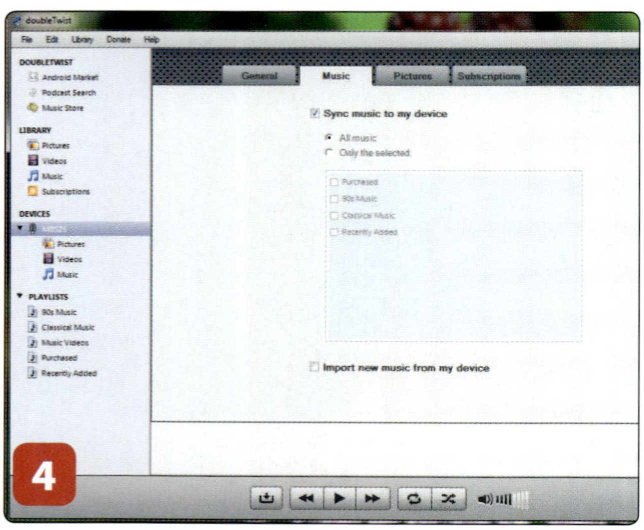

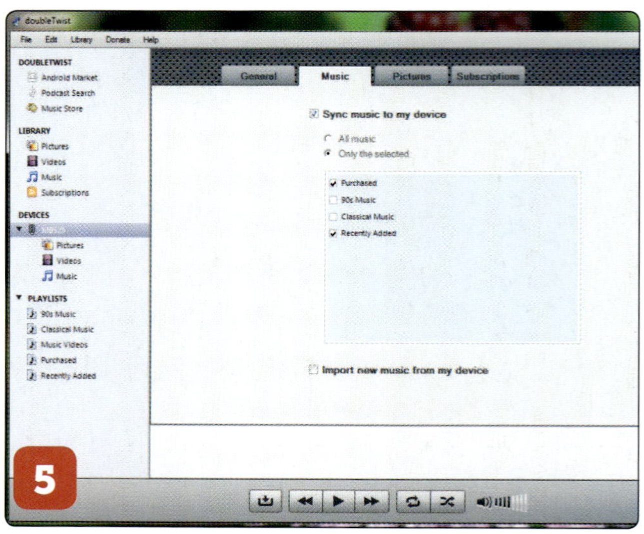

Home networking

Share your music and photos using the TwonkyServer app

Home networking fans may be familiar with Twonky (available from twonky.com). Support for Twonky servers has been included in media-sharing drives for many years. However, until recently, only Windows devices could take advantage of its likeable features. TwonkyServer Mobile for Google Android was launched in late 2010 and is free from Android Market.

Twonky is a universal plug-and-play (UPnP) and Digital Living Network Alliance (DLNA)-compliant service that searches for media stored on devices within a network. More commonly used to push content from a PC to a network-aware hard drive plugged into a TV, the latest version of Twonky allows content to be copied from one device to another and then be pushed to a third for playback. It's a bit like Windows Media Player's 'Play to' feature, which lets you send a downloaded podcast or music album to your Xbox 360 for playback.

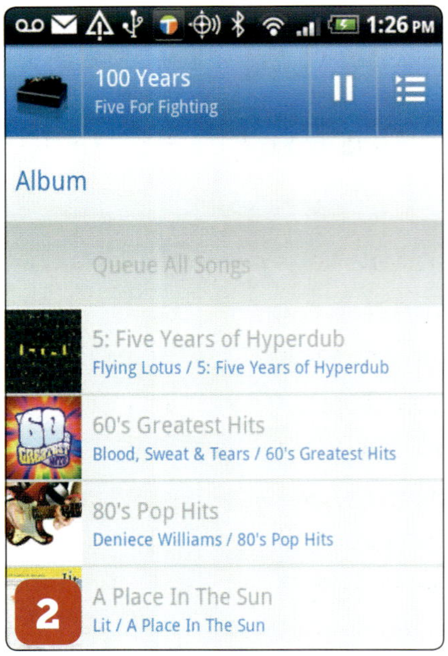

1 Getting started First off, download TwonkyServer Mobile on to your handset from the Android Market. A one-time setup routine sees the app search for available media devices, request confirmation of which you'd like to use, then display a list of content you can access. Your media is separated into Photos, Videos and Music folders.

2 Share your media Click on an item in your Twonky library and you'll be able to send it to another device on the ad-hoc network. Select an item such as a photo or music track and press Beam to send it to another device. You could, for example, have a track play on a network audio player such as a Logitech Squeezebox or Philips Streamium.

3 Picture show You can create a photo slideshow by selecting a whole folder of photos. Simply choose the images that you'd like to stream to a television or another display, and then click the clock icon at the bottom left to choose how quickly slideshow images are refreshed.

4 Play music To play a track or video clip on another device you first need to copy it to your tablet PC or smartphone. Select the device on which the item is stored, browse to the file and click the option to copy it. Now switch from the 'Play from' to the 'Play to' menu on the main screen and choose the destination device. Track details and album art will display at the bottom left of the TwonkyServer screen.

Taking and managing photos

Besides shooting pictures, it's easy to organise, view and share them

Who needs to carry a camera when a smartphone is at hand? The Android operating system packs so much functionality that it can often stand in for both a camera and a PC. Once you've learned how to harness your device's photo capabilities, capturing and sharing memorable moments is a snap.

▲ Tap the camera icon to set your Android camera to its still photo mode

THE ANDROID CAMERA

Most Android devices have a dedicated hardware button to start up the built-in camera. Alternatively, you can open it via the Camera app icon in the device's app launcher. (If you like, you can place this icon on your home screen as a shortcut.)

When you open the Android camera, you'll see a large viewfinder plus a few on-screen buttons. If you rotate your device horizontally, the uppermost button will be an icon for opening its gallery of stored photos. The next button down is a switch that toggles between the still photo and video recording modes. Finally, the round button at the bottom is the shutter – the button you touch to snap a picture or to begin recording video.

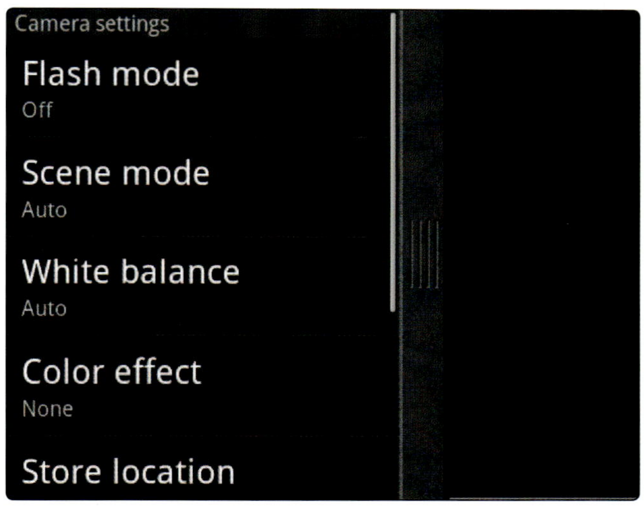

▲ Choose from a variety of custom shooting modes to pep up your pictures

In still photo mode, you can tap anywhere on the image in the viewfinder to zoom in or out. Tapping once will bring up the zoom controls, so you can zoom in small increments. Double-tapping (tapping your finger twice in quick succession, much as you'd double-click with a mouse) lets you quickly zoom all the way in or all the way out.

You can reach the camera's advanced options by hitting the Menu key and selecting options, or by touching the lined area to the far left of the screen. A slide-out menu will present you with

▲ **Having taken a photo, you can delete it, share it or set it as your background**

options for photo size, photo quality, and whether to store location information with the image.

Beginning with Android 2.0, the settings panel includes other advanced camera options: built-in flash support, customisable scene modes (action mode, night mode, and so on), white balance, colour effects and macro focus mode. Phones running Android 2.0 or higher also have an integrated digital zoom capability for magnifying an image to as much as four times its original size, although, unlike a zoom lens, this doesn't capture any extra detail.

VIEWING AND SHARING

You can use the Camera app to access images stored on your phone: just tap the small thumbnail image at the top left of the camera screen (the thumbnail always displays the most recent photo you've captured). When you load your images in this way, you'll first see your most recent photo displayed at full-screen size. Tapping your finger on the picture will enable you to zoom in or out; tapping your finger on the left or right side of the viewing area will let you move sequentially through the other stored images.

Buttons on the right of the screen provide quick ways to delete the image; to share it via Bluetooth, email, text message, Picasa, or any social networking app installed on your phone; and to set the image as your main system wallpaper or as an icon for someone in your contacts >

list. By hitting your device's Menu key, you'll gain options for rotating or cropping the image as well as for viewing detailed information about the file.

Another possibility is to view images directly from Android's Gallery app, accessible from the app launcher (and, again, available as a shortcut that you can place on your home screen). On loading the Gallery, you'll be able to browse your photos and videos in folders organised according to how and when you obtained them. Once you've opened a folder, you can tap any image to view it at full-screen size. You can then tap the enlarged photo to zoom in or to access other image management options.

The Gallery app allows you to play a slideshow of your photos, too. From inside a folder, tap the Menu key and select Slideshow to begin. To customise the slideshow, hit the Menu key and select Settings. There you'll find options for how long each image will remain on screen, what kind of transition will happen between images, and of course in what order the images will appear.

The Settings menu also contains options for altering the size and order of thumbnails displayed in the Gallery app.

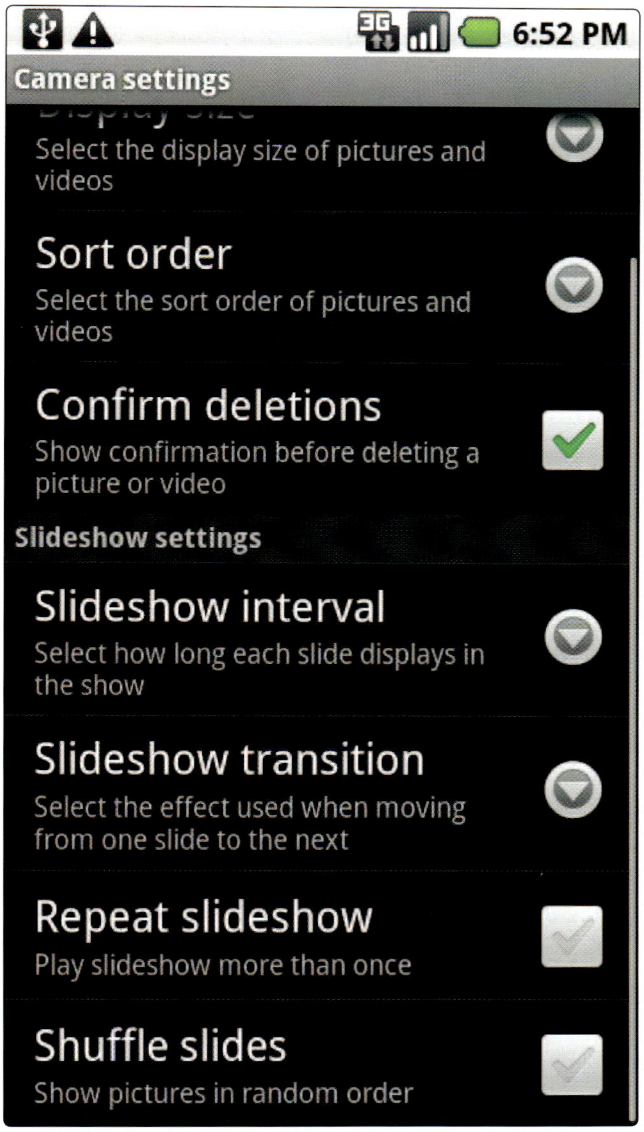

▲ **Your phone can display slideshows of your favourite photos. Click the option in the Gallery app and adjust the settings**

EDITING IMAGES

There's no default Google app for image editing in Android, but in the Android Market you'll find plenty of options for manipulating your pictures. Among the most advanced utilities is Adobe's free Photoshop Express app. As you'd expect, it's a far cry from the full desktop version of Photoshop, but the app makes it easy to perform essential operations such as cropping and colour correction and blurring of your images.

Another useful option is the PicSay Photo Editor. This free app includes tools for colour-correcting images and for adding visual effects, graphics, and word balloons. PicSay Pro (£2.63) adds a bevy

of additional photo-editing features, including painting tools, functions to cut out and paste parts of photos (such as transferring heads to new bodies) by multitouch, and cartoon speech bubbles.

If you like widgets, you'll be pleased at the number of photo-related programs that can bring images on to your desktop. Android has a built-in photo gallery widget that lets you place a single 2x2 inch photo on your home screen. The slightly more robust Androidlet Photo Widget (62p from the Android Market) lets you add live, cycling image galleries to your home screen in 1x1in, 2x2in and 3x3in sizes. You can customise how frequently the images rotate and what kind of frame surrounds them, and you can even set the widget to display images from Flickr, Picasa or other online photo storage services.

OTHER WAYS TO GET IMAGES

Besides using photos that you've snapped yourself, you can download images from the internet or transfer them to your Android phone or tablet from your computer. Any image you save to your device, regardless of exactly where you store it, will always be shown in the Gallery application.

To grab an image from the web, just press and hold your finger on it while in your device's web browser. A menu will pop up with the option to save the image.

To transfer an image from your computer, you can simply drag and drop it from your PC while your phone is connected to a USB port. Plug in the cable, then touch the notification area at the top of your device's screen. Tap USB connected in the notification area, then tap Mount to make your phone or tablet's memory appear as a storage device on your desktop (whether in Windows, Mac OS X or Linux). Photos you've taken on your device can be transferred to your computer in the same way.

▲ Adobe Photoshop Express (formerly Photoshop.com Mobile) is just one of the picture-editing apps available for Android

Improving your photos

Point-and-shoot is great, but there are ways to enhance your results

The cameras built into mobile phones used to be little more than a gimmick, with just a couple of megapixels and no frills. The images captured lacked the quality of those from even the most basic standalone camera. Fortunately, things have changed, and today's Android devices increasingly include cameras of 5Mp or more, with features such as LED flash and image stabilisation.

In fact, the standard of built-in cameras is now so good that you no longer have to kick yourself for leaving your digital camera at home when the occasion arises for a picture. Getting decent results every time, however, still depends on knowing a few tricks of the trade, so over the following pages we'll look at how to avoid – and create – blur, how to compensate for different lighting conditions using flash and ISO adjustment, and how to tag and organise photos on your PC to ensure that, once you've taken that perfect shot, it doesn't just languish on a memory card, never to see the light of day again.

1 Flash Even in bright sunlight, it can be effective in providing a burst to compensate for sharp shadows and underexposure. The flash punches up details only when you're within a few feet, so stay close to your subject.

2 Adjust ISO setting When shooting at night, increasing the ISO setting can be more effective than using the flash. Don't crank up the ISO too far, though, or you'll end up with digital noise (randomly lighter or darker pixels, creating a speckled effect reminiscent of film grain) in your shots.

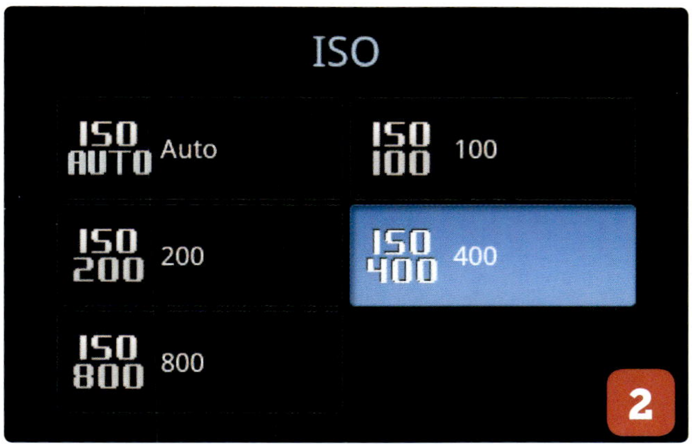

▲ **A higher ISO setting will capture more detail in lower light, though it risks 'noise'**

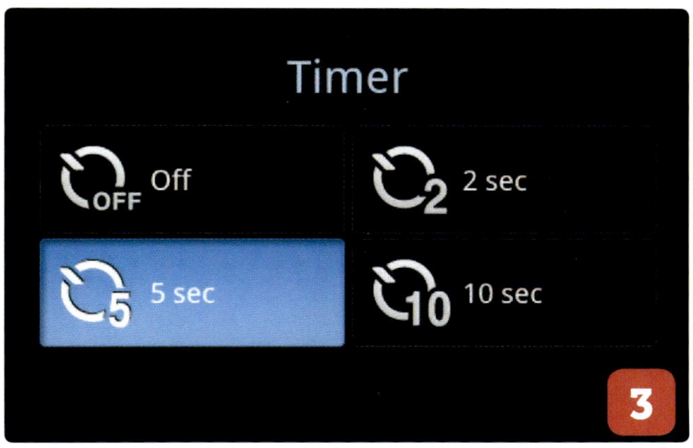

▲ **If your device has a camera self-timer, it's handy for snapping yourself**

You can alter the ISO in the main camera settings menu. When you're ready to take a photo, turn on the image stabiliser if your device has this feature.

3 Keep still! Thanks to autofocus, your shots shouldn't be blurred unless something is going wrong. Camera shake is the most likely suspect, so hold your device with both hands, and keep your elbows tucked into the sides of your body for support. When you press the shutter button, make no other movement until the image has been taken. If you're shooting in ample light, try increasing the shutter speed, if there's an option for that, or increase the ISO setting (as above), which will force the camera to automatically increase the shutter speed to prevent over-exposure. Selecting the Sports mode has a similar effect. A faster shutter means less time for wobbles to occur.

4 Fake bokeh Blur can sometimes be used to advantage, pulling an in-focus subject out of a softer background. When it's created using depth of field (where only objects at a certain distance are in focus) it's known as 'bokeh'. This is hard to achieve with a smartphone camera, but another way is to follow a moving subject. Try focusing on a friend as you walk along together, keeping them in the same position in the frame as you move; when you take the shot, the background will be softened by motion blur while your friend is in focus. This effect works best with a slower shutter (more time to create blur), so avoid Sports mode, use a low ISO and turn off flash.

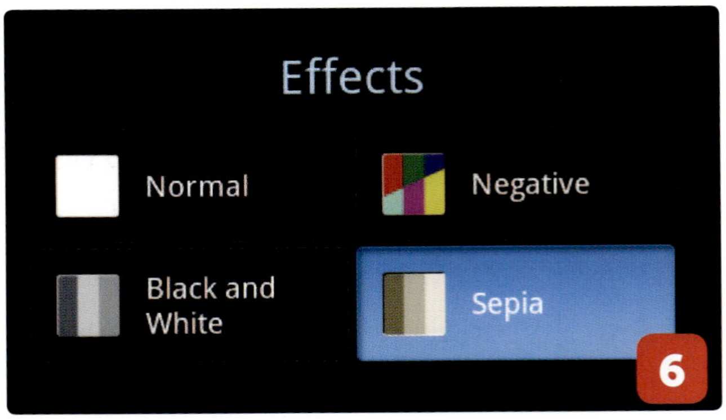

▲ **Special effects can liven up any photo, but even better is applying your own creativity, such as picking an arty angle**

5 Use a timer The self-timer is a useful function for shooting without camera shake as well as for including yourself in the frame. For example, the Samsung Galaxy S's timer is accessible in the Camera, Settings menu. If your handset doesn't have a timer, third-party apps can help: try Camera Zoom FX from the Android Market. This timer gives you up to 10 seconds to get into the shot once you've pressed the capture button.

6 Add effects Under Camera, Settings, Effects, you'll find a number of filters you can apply, such as Sepia. These can be fun and help to mask any shortcomings in image quality. To get more creative, an effective trick is to shoot from an unusual perspective: try capturing a group shot from a low angle after your team conquers a mountain, for example,

7 Get up close One final and essential piece of advice when shooting with a small, low-resolution camera that has no optical zoom: always make the effort to get close to your subject. It pays dividends.

Organising your images

Keep track of your snaps with built-in and add-on metadata tools

Taking pictures is pointless unless you look at them later. That in turn means organising your photos so you can quickly view the ones you want. Tags make relatively light work of this organisational process and mean items you later want to retrieve can be found more easily. Naming photos as you go is good practice, but not every app you may use on your Android device will allow you to do so. Transferring shots to a PC for tagging can be easier.

1 View tags 'Metadata' is information stored along with an image, such as the camera used, the exposure and, most importantly, any tags (keywords) associated with it. Apps such as ASTRO can tag selected items, but for faster batch-tagging import your photos to your PC from your Android device. If you have a suitable microSD card adaptor, you can plug it in directly.

2 Add a tag Label the photo folder, then click on any photo and press the Tags field at the foot of the Windows Explorer window. Type in a descriptive term; you can enter multiple tags separated by semicolons. To later find this or similar photos, click the Explorer search field and

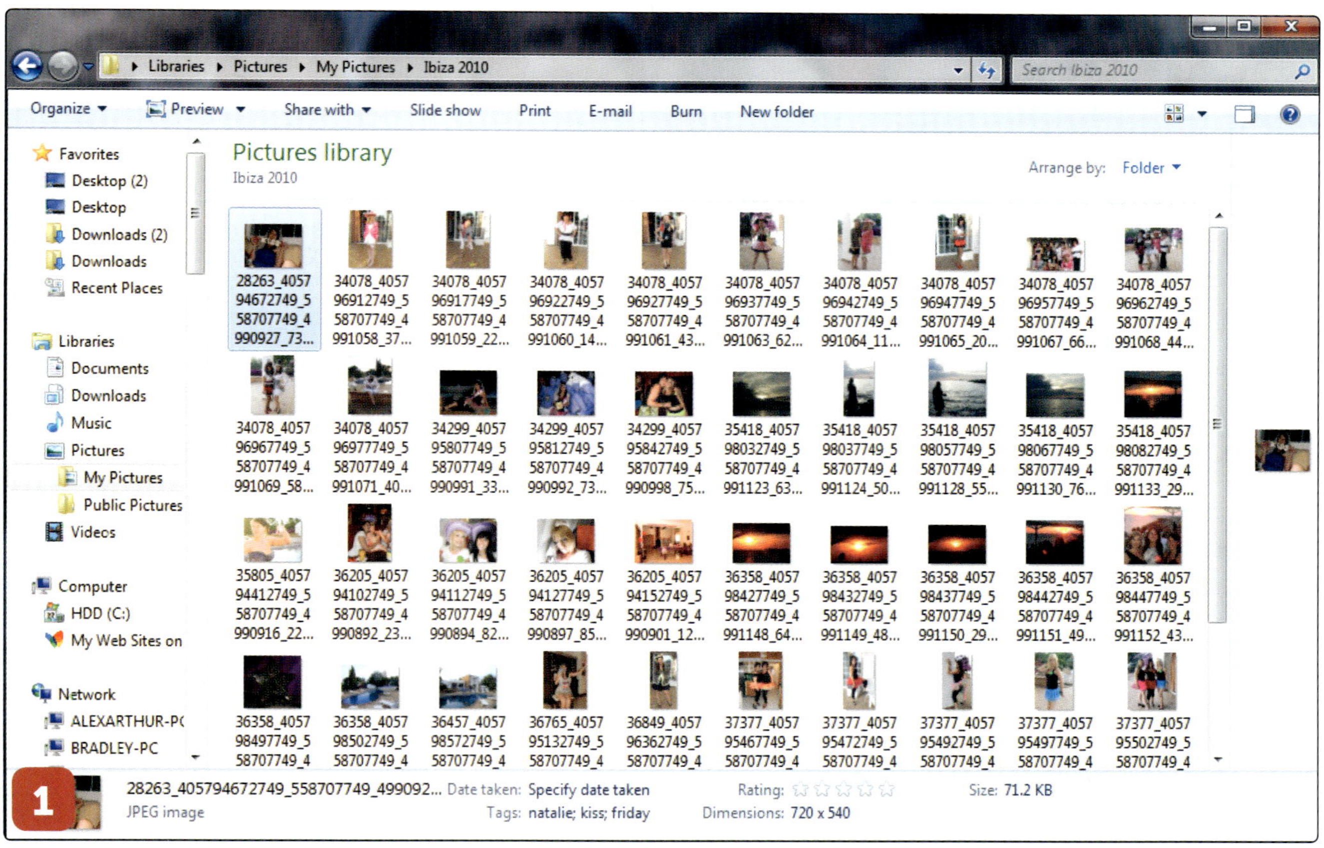

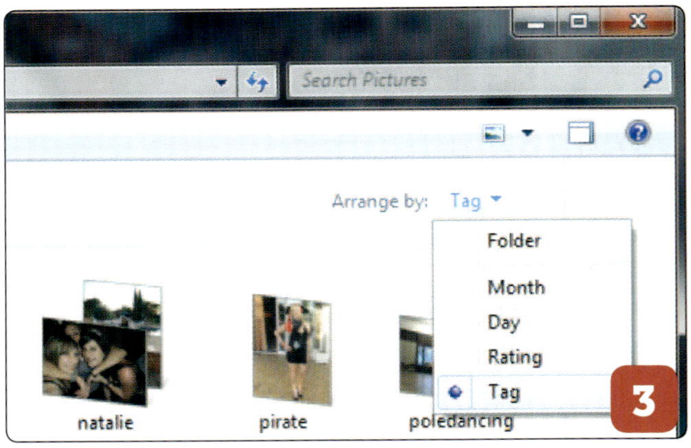

enter 'tag: x', replacing 'x' with one of the keywords you entered as tags.

3 Arrange by tag Alternatively, open your photo library and select Tag from the Arrange by menu. A list of available tags and thumbnails of associated images will appear. Select the tag you want. To see file information, including the number of pictures with that tag, right-click any blank spot within the folder and select View, Details from the contextual menu.

4 Share shots on Photo Gallery For more photo tagging tools, try the free Windows Live Photo Gallery (download it from tinyurl.com/2bh6x67). This lets you batch-convert photos, make quick fixes, add tags and share images on Flickr, YouTube and Facebook. Once you've got an account, you'll be able to upload shots straight from your Android device for sharing and online storage too. You'll need to enter your Windows Live ID, or register one if you're not already signed up. The app trawls your hard drive and displays all the images it finds. Click an image to view its tags. To add a tag, edit the information on the right. Click under Descriptive tags, enter keywords and hit Return. You can also add 'People tags': the app finds any faces in the image and lets you put a name to each.

5 Add ratings and captions You can also give each photo a caption. Again, click a photo and adjust the metadata. To search for a set of tagged images, enter your keyword in the search box; to search for multiple tags separate each keyword from the next with a forward slash (/).

6 Fix photos Windows Live Essentials Photo Gallery also lets you make basic edits. Select an image and click Fix at the top of the window. Options then appear at the right-hand side to let you adjust the picture's colour and exposure, crop or straighten it, sharpen up detail, fix red-eye, or turn the photo black and white.

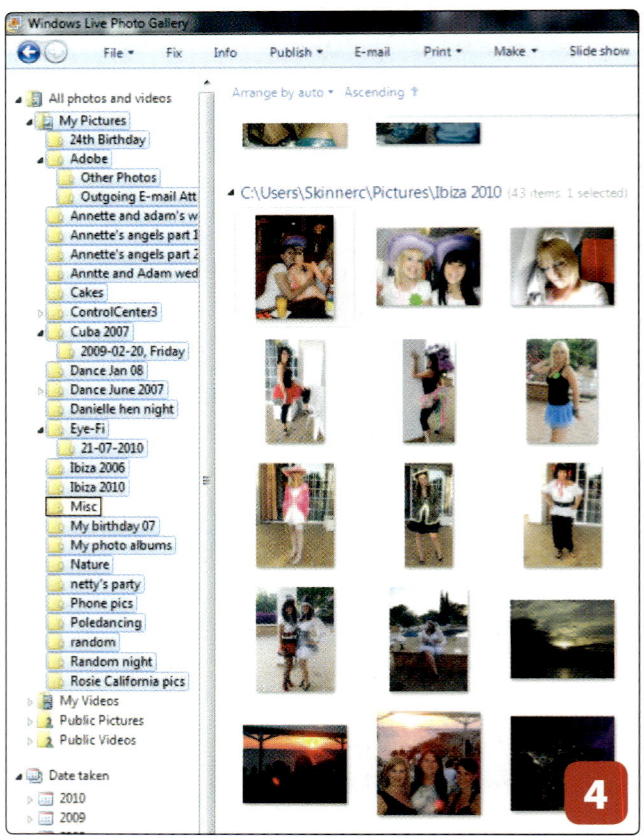

Create, share and play video

Your Android device also has a talent for moving pictures

Whether you've got movie-making ambitions or just want to capture a few precious moments, your Android device can help you grab plenty of footage and share it with the world.

LIGHTS, CAMERA... PHONE?

To start shooting footage in Android, launch the Camera app and toggle it to Video mode by tapping the small camcorder/camera switch on the right side of the screen. Note that, unlike when shooting stills, it's important to hold the phone horizontally – in landscape orientation – at this point, since there's no such thing as portrait mode for video.

Your camera's default settings should give you usable results, automatically setting focus and exposure while compensating for varying lighting conditions. You can fine-tune your video capture, however, by hitting the Menu button on your phone and choosing Settings. Here you'll find options for adjusting the quality, maximum duration, white balance and colour effects.

Most of the time you'll be shooting at high quality, which can quickly take up space on your device's SD card. However, if you're planning to share your videos via MMS messaging, it makes more sense to shoot them at low quality to make sure they'll be small enough to send.

Auto white balance is enabled by default, and usually delivers realistic tones, but if you're planning to shoot a number of clips in one location, it's better to select the white balance manually.

When you're happy with your settings, tap the red Record button on the

▶ Tap the switch in Android's Camera app to switch between shooting still images and video clips

screen to start capturing. And when you're done, tap the same button to save the recording to your memory card.

PUTTING ON A SHOW

To share videos from your phone, simply tap them in the Gallery to open them. Tap and hold a video until the context menu pops up, and select Share to view a list of apps that can send your video to friends. You should see options such as Gmail, Messaging (for MMS), Twidroid (for Twitter) and YouTube.

Bear in mind that certain methods of sharing video will have limitations. As mentioned above, if you want to share your videos with friends via MMS, it's best to shoot in low quality and to keep the message shorter than 30 seconds.

For instant sharing, you can opt to start recording video from within Android's Messaging app. To do this, tap Messaging in the app menu, select a recipient, then hit the Menu button on your phone and choose Attach. Next, choose Capture video. By default, Messaging will set your recording quality to Low and give you a 30-second countdown timer to help you limit your clip to an appropriate length. If you're not happy with your footage, you can tap the Retake button and try again. When you're satisfied, tap OK; Messaging will then convert your video into MMS format. Finally, tap Send to fire it off.

PLAYING MOVIES AND MORE

For entertainment on the go, you can copy video files to your phone and play them back anytime. A free utility called Videora (tinyurl.com/34jwrlg) runs on your Windows PC or Mac to convert DVDs and other movie content into a format that will play on various Android phones. Bear in mind that a full-length movie can take more than an hour to convert.

Alternatively, HandBrake (handbrake.fr) can also convert movies to assorted formats. If you choose this as your video conversion tool, try a free Android Market download called LukLuk to play a wide variety of video formats, including MP4 and WMA. If you register this app, you can also access a selection of premium streaming movies and TV content.

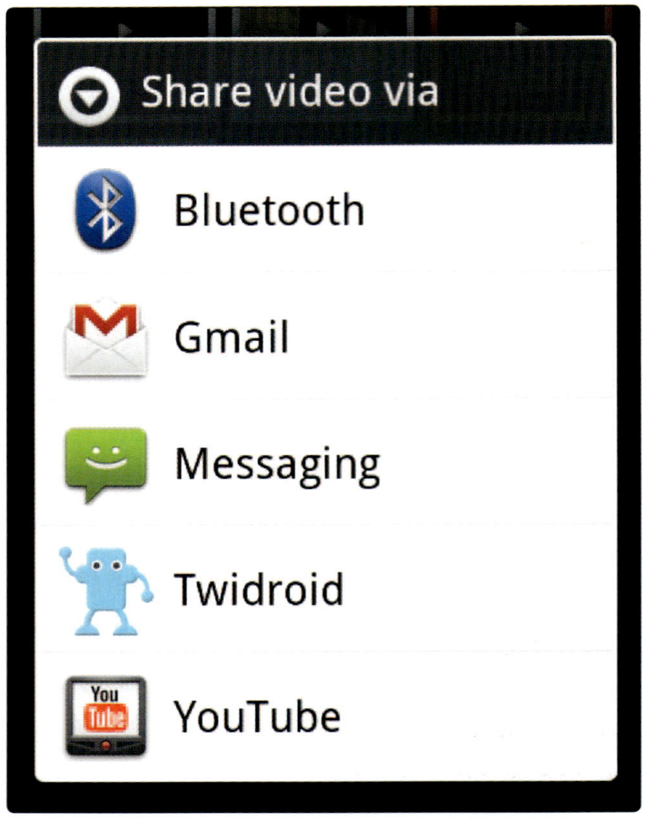

▲ You can share your videos straight from Android through a variety of social messaging and online service apps

Use BBC iPlayer on Android

Catch up with your favourite BBC shows on your Android device

The BBC iPlayer is a free app for your Android device. It allows you to watch catch-up TV, some movies and even live television as it's broadcast. You can also use it to pick up BBC radio. You should note that iPlayer requires Android 2.2 or higher, and won't play on earlier versions of the OS.

If the iPlayer isn't already on your Android smartphone, download it from the Market. Just search for 'BBC iPlayer' and then follow the installation steps. The process takes just a few seconds. Now you'll find the BBC iPlayer in the apps list. Tap and hold to copy it on to the home page of your Android device.

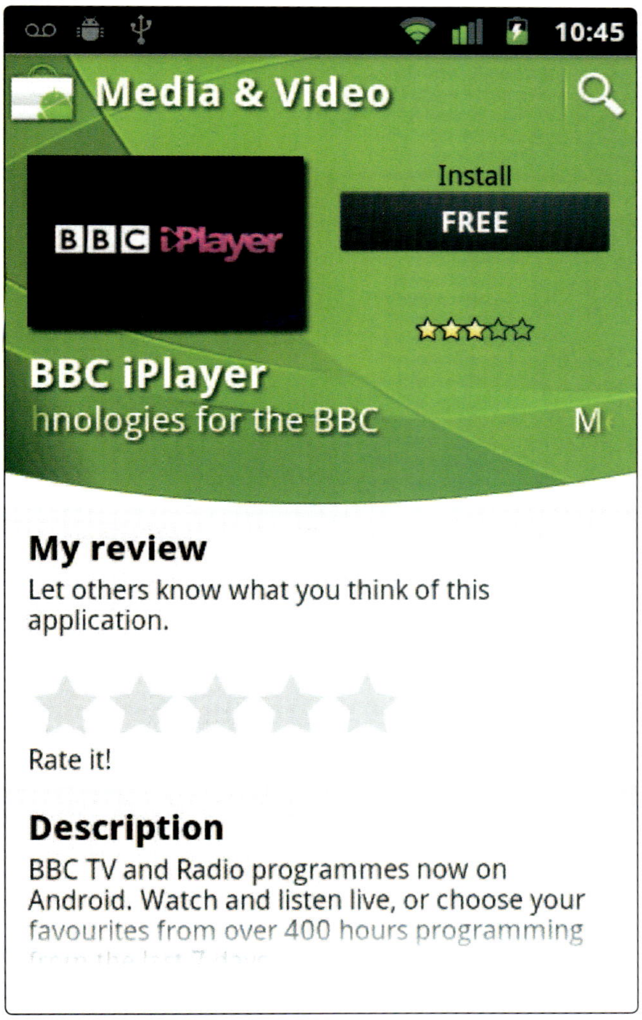

▲ You can download the BBC iPlayer for free from the Android Market

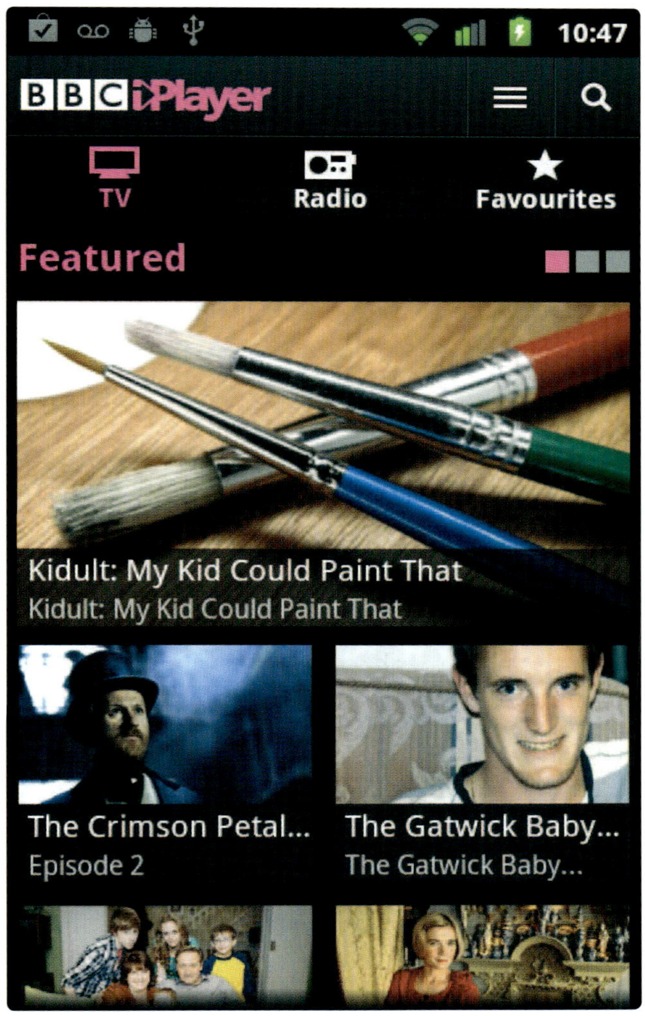

▲ The icons at the top of the screen let you switch between radio and TV shows

The BBC iPlayer streams media to your Android device over the air, so you may prefer to use it over Wi-Fi where possible rather than over your 3G data account. If so, before running the app, make sure you are connected to Wi-Fi.

When you first use the BBC iPlayer, it may tell you that you need the Flash Player installed. Just click 'Download now' and you'll be taken to the relevant part of the Market to complete the download.

WHAT'S ON THE BOX

Back in the BBC iPlayer note the icons towards the top of the screen for TV, Radio and Favourite. TV is selected by default. If you tap Radio, the main screen will change to show radio programmes. Scroll down to see more radio or TV shows, and tap something to start streaming it. If you tap a TV programme, tap 'play in full screen' to see it in widescreen. Tap the screen at any time to access the playback controls.

To search for a particular television or radio programme, simply tap the Search button top-right corner of the main screen and type in your search terms. Then hit the magnifying glass next to the search box. Wait while your search results are retrieved, then scroll through the search results and tap whatever takes your fancy to start watching it.

There is another way to refine the full range of programmes available in the BBC iPlayer. Tap the icon to the left of the search icon and you can browse by category and by channel, and see what's showing on Live TV. This is the easiest way to find any movies that are available on the iPlayer as they have their own category.

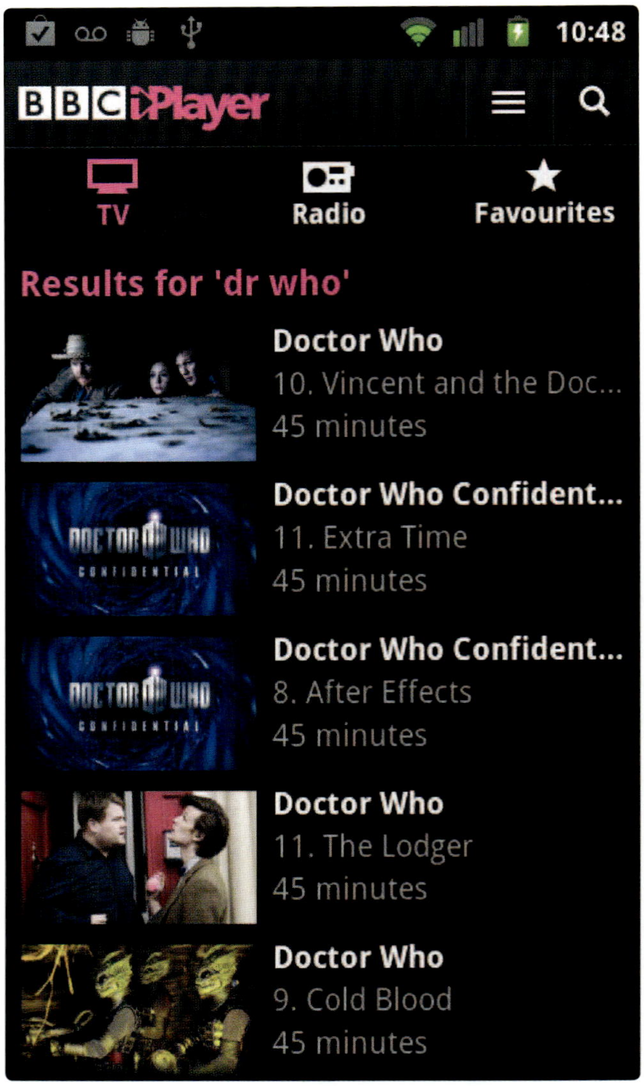

▲ Tap the magnifying glass icon to search for your favourite programmes

You can also make a programme a favourite by checking that box while it's playing or long pressing on it in a listing. Then when new episodes of favourite programmes appear they'll be listed on the Favourites page. This is handy as you can watch the episodes that are due to expire soonest first.

Call **01858 438 867** and quote ANDR

• Save 83 per cent • Be the first to read Macworld

and save 83%

Message from the Editor

The very first issue of Macworld was published back in 1984, just as Apple launched the first Mac. Since then Macworld has followed Apple religiously. We've been there at every Expo, every product launch, we've had our hands on every new piece of kit, we've been with Apple through the highs and the lows. We know Apple. Macworld is created by an international team of experts based in London and San Francisco, who live, eat and dream Apple.

Our contributors include specialists who use Macs at work: designers and illustrators, professional photographers, animators, musicians, developers and more.

If you are new to Apple and are looking for advice to help you get started, or if you are a Mac fanatic looking to justify your next buy, Macworld is the magazine to ensure you make the right decision. And then we'll help you get the most out of the world's best computer, to be more productive and creative than you ever thought possible.

Join the Macworld team every issue as we analyse the latest product announcements from the world's biggest (and still the best) technology company.

Karen Haslam, editor@macworld.co.uk

Macworld Social

We're a pretty social bunch here at Macworld, and we're happy to chat to readers. You can email us on team@macworld.co.uk or use any of these social networks…

www.facebook.com/macworlduk

www.twitter.com/macworlduk

http://lnkd.in/GQgUU7

www.macworld.co.uk/forum

TERMS & CONDITIONS

- No obligation – we'll give you a full refund on any unmailed issues if you ever decide to cancel
- After three issues for £3 Macworld subscription will continue at the discounted rate of £49.99 for 14 issues
- For subscribers paying by cheque or credit card, subscription rate is £54.99 for 12 months
- You'll receive 14 issues in a 12-month subscription
- Your subscription will start with the next available issue
- For overseas rates please call +44 1858 438 867 and quote reference ANDR

Beyond the basics

Chapter 4

Chapter 4

Beyond the basics

An Android device is home to not only your music and app collection, but also personal information that you wouldn't want falling into the wrong hands. With this in mind, we look at Android's built-in security features and what to do if your smartphone or tablet goes missing. We also show you how to erase data before you get rid of an old Android device. Finally, we examine the best ways to keep in touch with friends and family using the most popular social networking apps.

Secure your Android device

When your mobile goes missing, find it before others find your data

Whether you paid a small fortune for the hottest Android device or got it for 'free' with a modest contract, it's a good bet that the data stored on your mobile is at least as valuable as the hardware itself. If your phone or tablet is ever lost or stolen, you'll either be glad you took precautions to protect all your content, or you'll sorely wish you had. In this article, we'll walk you through setting up Android's built-in security tools and suggest a few third-party extras that can add valuable safeguards for your personal information.

LOCK OUT PRYING EYES

Unlike most other mobile handsets, which use alphanumeric passcodes to prevent interlopers from messing with your data, Android introduces a novel

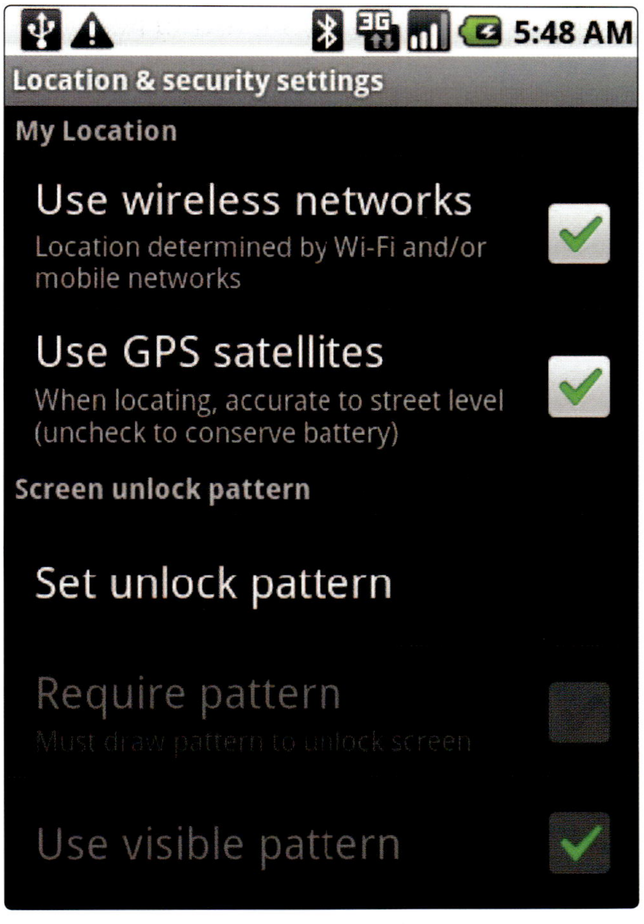

▲ **Setting an unlock pattern gives your device a first line of physical defence**

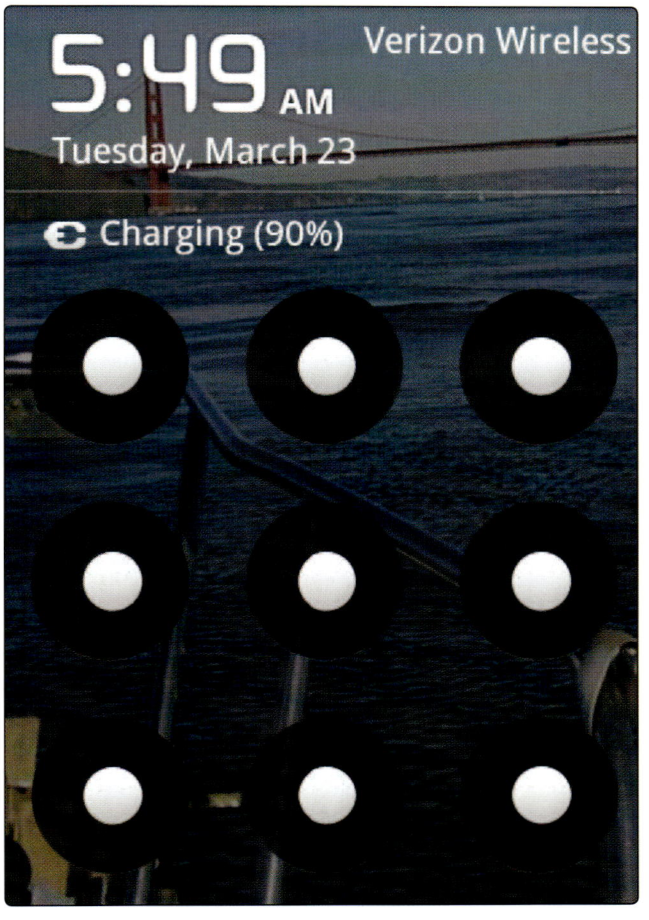

▲ **When idle, the screen will display the dots ready to accept a pattern**

system called an unlock pattern. Rather than punch in a code on a keypad, you swipe your fingertip across the screen in a pre-specified pattern, connecting a series of dots along the way. If the pattern you swipe matches the pattern that's been previously entered into the device's memory, the operating system unlocks. If not, try again.

Like a passcode, the security of an unlock pattern is directly related to the number of data points it contains. Just as a six-digit code is likely to be safer than a four-digit one, a pattern connecting six dots will be harder to break than one with only four dots. (And four is the minimum number for any Android unlock pattern.)

To set an unlock pattern, open the Settings menu and tap Location & security. If you haven't set one before, you'll see Set unlock pattern listed under Screen unlock pattern. If there's already an unlock pattern in place, it'll say Change unlock pattern. In either case, tap that option to get to the Draw an unlock pattern screen. (If you already have a pattern entered, you'll need to confirm it before creating a new one.)

You can begin drawing your new unlock pattern by touching your finger on any dot on the screen, then swiping over nearby dots, without lifting your finger off the surface, to connect them in any pattern you choose. Remember, that more complex patterns will be more secure than simple ones, so the more dots you connect, the better. If you just connect four dots in a simple L shape, for example, the first nefarious character to happen upon your device will be pretty sure to get into it.

Unfortunately, convenience and security can sometimes be mutually exclusive, and this is definitely one of those cases. If you really want to keep your stuff safe, don't wimp out on the unlock pattern. On the other hand, don't create a pattern so complicated you can never get it right yourself.

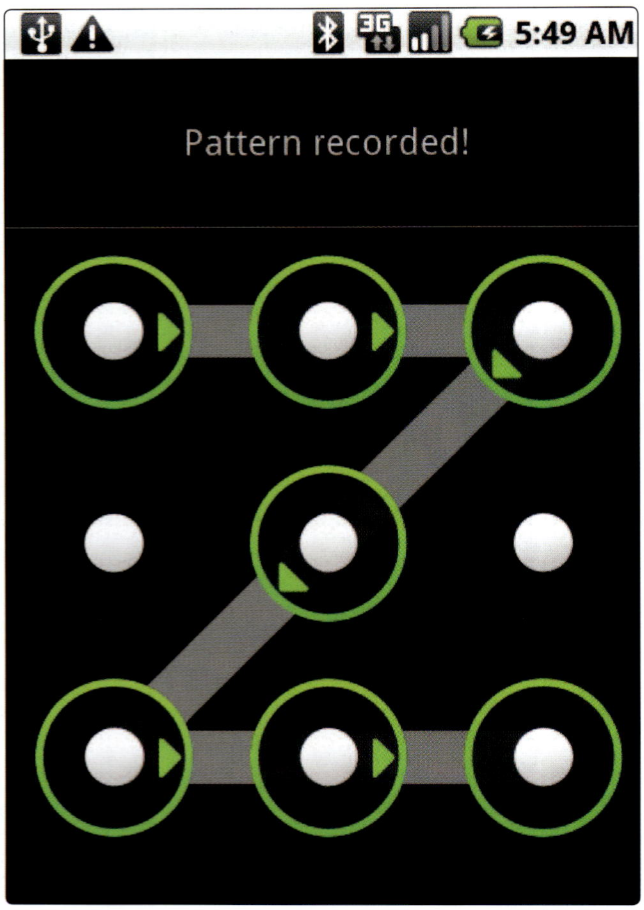

▲ **Drag your finger over the dots in the correct pattern to unlock the device**

FIND YOUR PHONE

Whether you've let it slip it between the sofa cushions, left it on a restaurant table or had it stolen out of your car, a missing ›

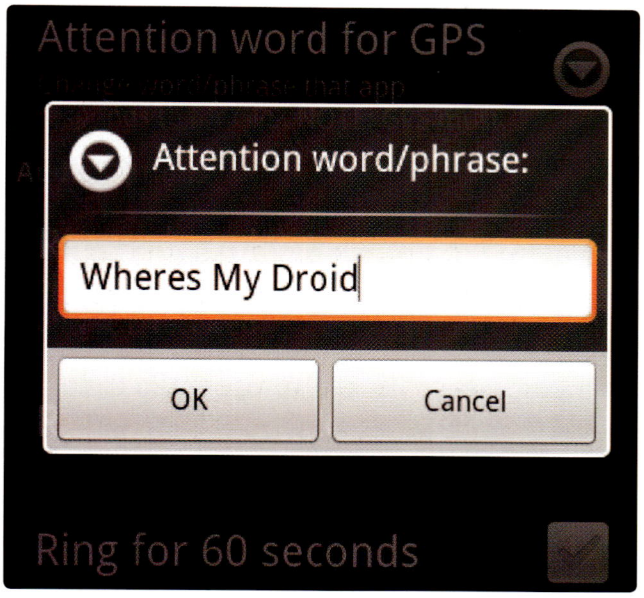

▲ **When the Where's My Droid app receives your 'attention word' in a text, it will either sound off an alarm or text back its geographic position so you can find it**

mobile can be hard to recover. Fortunately, Android's built-in GPS functions can make it easy to find a device that's gone AWOL, as long as you're running the right software. The Android Market offers several good apps for tracking down a missing handset.

One of the simplest location trackers for Android is called Where's My Droid (free from the Android Market, or with extra features in return for a donation). This simple GPS-driven app lets you create a secret 'attention word' or passphrase that you can send to your device as a text message. When received, this will trigger a 'find me' mode.

After your phone goes missing, you'll have two options. If you think it's nearby, you can text your standard attention word to trigger a loud ring that, unlike simply dialling your own number, will always be audible, even if you left your ringtone set to silent. Alternatively, text your GPS 'attention word' and the device will send back a message stating its exact latitude and longitude, so you can make your way there and pick it up.

While an app like this won't do anything to protect your data from theft, it does make it less likely that a mislaid mobile will disappear forever.

ADVANCED SECURITY

For more robust security options coupled with the ability to track down your device, two apps stand out. McAfee WaveSecure (www.wavesecure.com, $19.90 per year, see page 108) and Mobile Defense (www.mobiledefense.com) both give you the ability to locate your phone from a secure website, so you can not only get the GPS coordinates of your device but see it on a map. Again, these services let you set off an alarm that will make the device easy to find if you're in earshot.

If your Android phone is truly lost, WaveSecure and Mobile Defense both offer additional tools to help you get it back. With each, you can remotely lock or unlock your device to either prevent thieves from getting into the operating system or to enable a good Samaritan to get in if so desired.

More importantly, you can use these apps to remotely back up and then wipe all your personal data from the device if nobody turns it in – so you can not only get your latest data back, but also protect it from falling into the wrong hands.

Erase data from your handset

Before you get rid of an old phone ensure that your data is removed

A report in March highlighted the sheer amount of data that is now routinely stored on our smartphones and how little heed some of us pay to what happens to our personal information. Security researchers bought dozens of phones and SIM cards from sites such as eBay and unearthed personal information on almost every one. However, when asked, most of us state that we ensure we wipe our phones before passing them on to a new owner or abandoning an older handset in favour of a faster, shinier new model.

The problem is, it's not simply a question of deleting all your contacts and text messages. Accounts that are set up for synchronisation and the trail of websites you've visited tell their own tale too. Here we look at how to prepare your Android device for retirement or a new owner by ensuring you've removed all traces of your own use – and checked for any photos or videos you want to keep.

TOO CLEVER BY HALF

You might think phone hacking and data theft from mobile phones is limited to

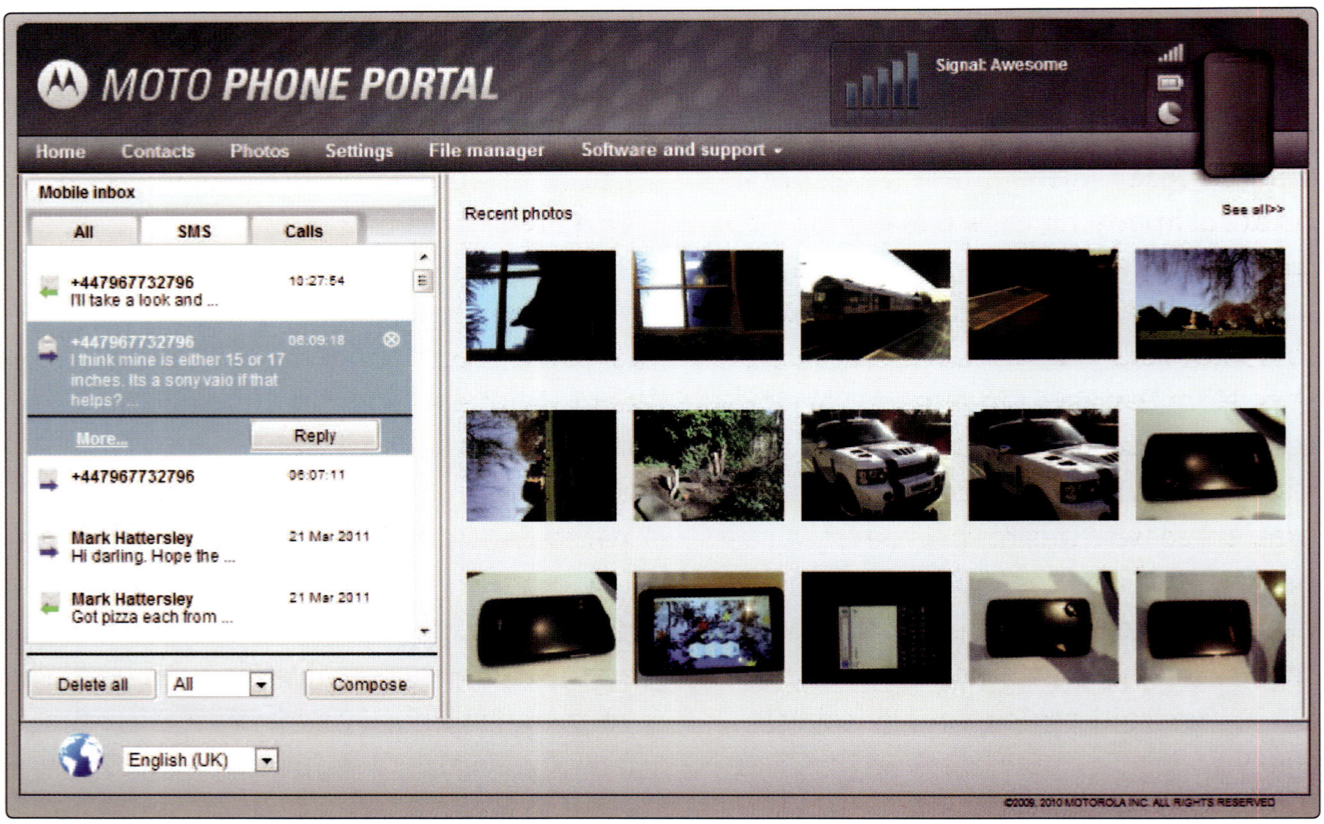

▲ **Text messages can be accessed by simply pugging a smartphone into a PC**

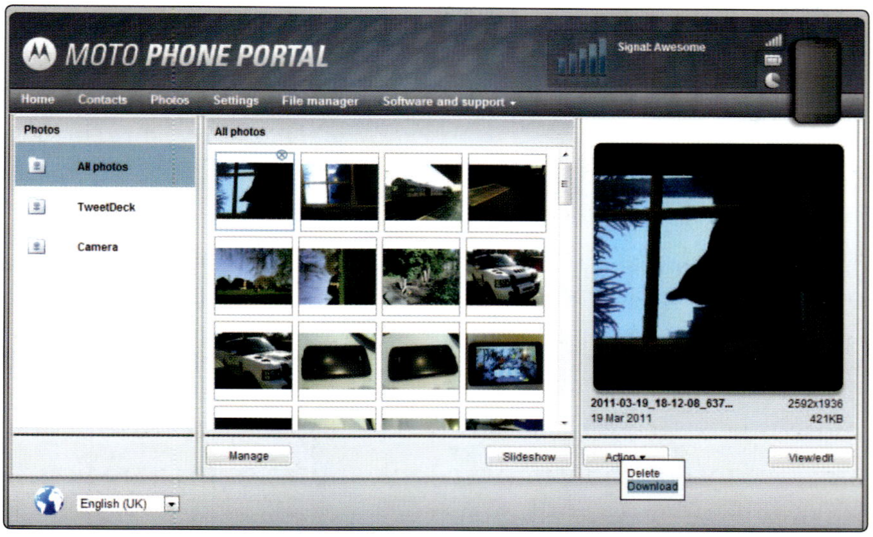

▲ **Delete photos individually to ensure you get them all**

royalty and celebrities, but unlocking its secrets is often as simple as plugging a phone in to a PC and watching what the media manager pops up. Let's just say we surprised ourselves by accidentally uncovering our own long-forgotten messages and call logs this way.

With media-management tools increasingly being stored on the devices to which they relate, rather than supplied on accompanying CDs, possession of a handset often delivers up most of its secrets. If nothing else, you need to PIN-protect access in case of loss.

Note that there are utilities available on the web that allow both hapless users who have deleted content in error and scammers with design on your details to uncover even deleted SIM card content, but a PIN code (for the SIM rather than the handset) can often deny them access. On an Android device this option is in the Settings, Location & security, Set up SIM card lock menu. You can also set up security governing access to the Secure Digital card or USB storage devices.

You should be aware of just how much information someone could glean just by plugging in a smartphone to a PC. Everything from web addresses to text message conversations and tweets is still logged. Since Motorola supports Device Stage for Windows 7, all that's needed is a USB cable to access all this data.

Rigorously go through the settings for each aspect of your Android smartphone to be sure that you have everything you need. Here, we've downloaded photos one by one and deleted each in turn, just to be sure we've got everything we want. However, you can also import photos and other files using the auto-import option in Windows. Note that in order to drag-and-drop content from your Android device you may first need to enable the handset as a mass storage device. This option should appear when you plug in the smartphone to your PC.

UNWELCOME ASSOCIATIONS

The other way of deleting what's on your phone is to use the tools on the device to do the job. Performing a factory reset lets you wipe absolutely everything, but this isn't always the best option. If you don't want to lose the apps you've bought or have another reason to preserve some of

Total wipeout

The Device Stage allows us to delete our browsing history as well as photos and call records – a check you might not otherwise get round to performing. Click the Confirm option to get rid of all those private messages. Note that if your phone is stolen you may be able to get the operator or manufacturer to put a lock on it, so its contents can't be read by a stranger. To be sure, plan ahead, and download and install one of the security tools offered on the Android Market. Some offer remote wiping, while others let you remotely lock up your device or will automatically bar access to someone if they don't enter the right security credentials. If you routinely push work files to and fro using your Android device, using such a utility should be a priority.

the contents – perhaps a family member is getting the handset and you're happy for them to use the apps but not to access your linked Facebook account – you need to enter Android's settings menus.

Click the Settings menu on the Android home screen and, under the Accounts and sync settings menu, scroll down to the Auto-sync options and check for any that have been set up for your social networking accounts. Under the Manage accounts sub-menu you'll see the current status for your Gmail, Facebook and Twitter accounts.

If you've removed the SIM card from the device in preparation for your change to a new handset, any associated accounts should be set to Off. Confusingly, if you click on Privacy, you'll be taken to the option to remove the account link from your device as well as to initiate a manual synchronisation.

▶ **You can back up your data, reinstall an app or erase all data on your phone**

To perform a factory reset, go to the Settings menu and choose SD & phone storage. Click on the option at the bottom labelled Factory data reset and confirm that you're happy to wipe the device.

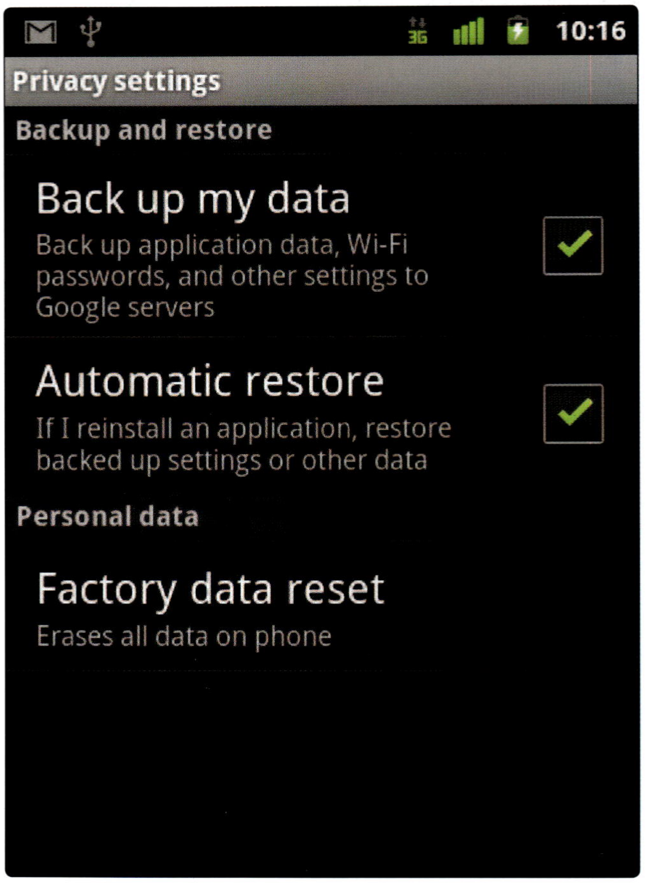

Make cheaper calls

Truphone and Vonage let you phone friends over the internet

Why pay for voice minutes on your smartphone tariff when everything else is carried over the mobile data connection? It's a good question, and the answer is you don't have to, if you install one of the growing number of apps that lets you make calls using VoIP (voice over internet protocol). Calls to users of compatible services are free, subject to your data plan, and even those to phones get cheaper. We'll take a look at a UK-based option, Truphone.

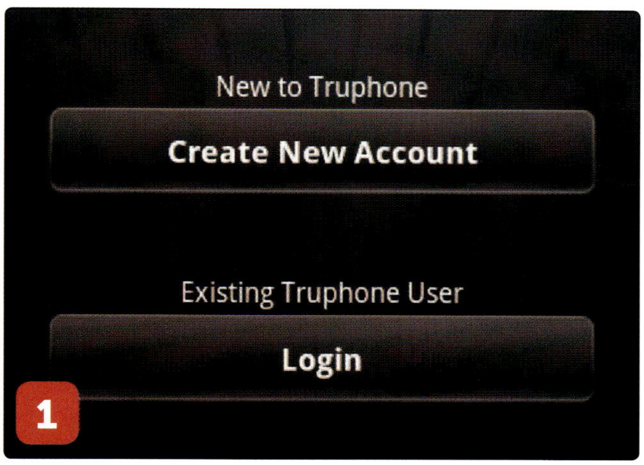

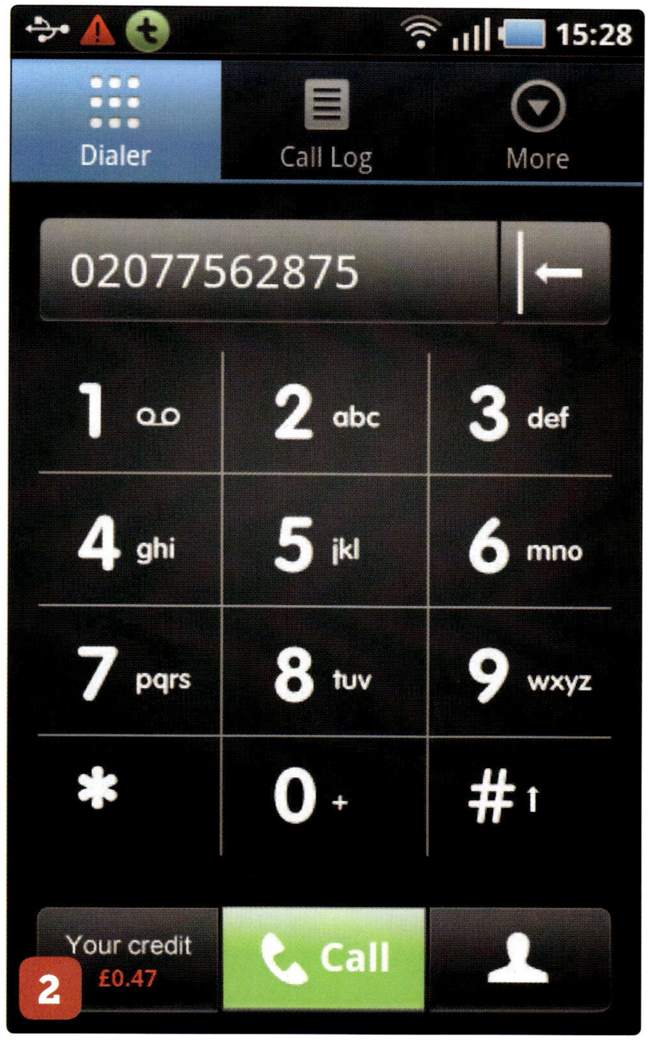

1 Install the app To get started, download the Truphone app (it's free) from the Android Market and click Install. Launch the app and click Create New Account. Give yourself a username and password, enter a valid email address, then click Create. You may get a warning stating that the app hasn't been tested for your handset and some functions may not work correctly. Click OK to continue.

2 Dial a number The Truphone Dialler presents you with a touchscreen mobile phone-style keypad like the one you'd normally use to make voice calls. Dial a number by touching the 'keys', or select someone from your contacts list and press the green Call button. Truphone routes the call over the internet, so calls to regular phone numbers work out cheaper than a standard call on most networks, especially

for international. You'll need to sign up with Truphone and buy credit; remaining credit is displayed in the bottom left corner of the screen and is adjusted after each call ends.

3 Free Wi-Fi calls You can call other Truphone users (along with those of compatible services including Skype and Google Talk) for free when your device is connected to the internet via Wi-Fi. Click on the number field in the Dialler to access the on-screen keypad. Use this to enter the Truphone username of the person you want, then tap Call. Note, however, that we found no way of identifying which of your contacts are on Truphone. You'll need to ask them for their username and enter it here.

4 Other VoIP services To contact Skype and Google Talk users over a Wi-Fi connection in the same way, you just need to add these accounts to your list of IM services within the Truphone app (above).

5 Add VoIP contacts Select More from the top right-hand side of the Dialler screen and choose the IM option. From the Services tab, select Add IM Service to display the screen shown here (right) and choose one of the four options from the drop-down menu: MSN, AIM, Skype or Google Talk (only the latter two currently support voice). After entering your username and password, tap Add IM Service. Under the Services tab, you'll now see an icon for the service you just added and an option to sign out. Select the IM tab to see your contacts from the added services, with those currently available highlighted in green. >

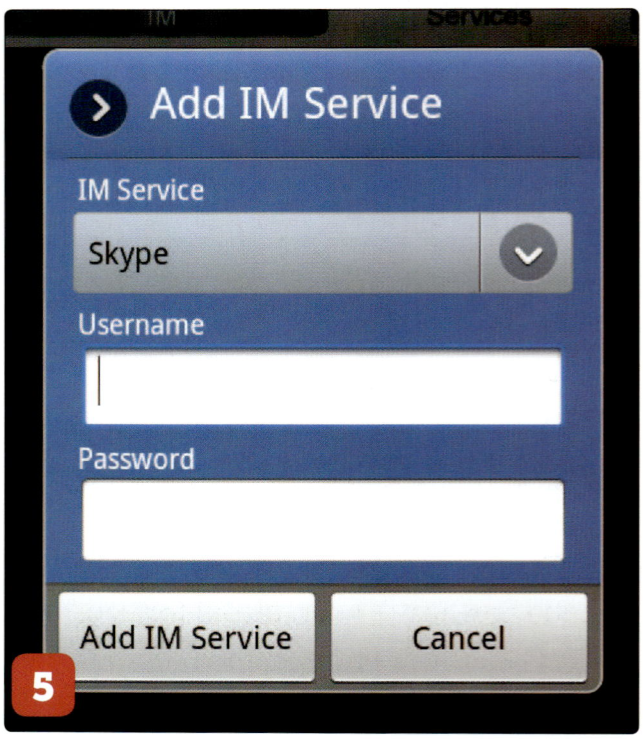

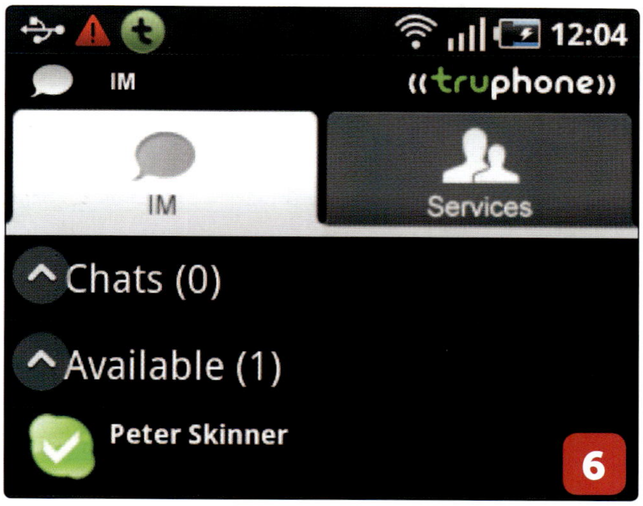

6 Start talking To call one of your available Skype or Google friends, click on a contact name. A text box and onscreen keyboard will pop up to let you type and send them an instant message. Alternatively, hit your device's Menu button to bring up the option to call them. Tap the Call option and Truphone will initiate the phone call.

7 International calls Truphone also offers cheaper long-distance calls. Truphone Anywhere redirects you to a local access number which completes your call via Truphone's server. When you dial, the screen shows 'Setting up the call' and a voice explains you'll be using Truphone Anywhere; hang up if you don't want to.

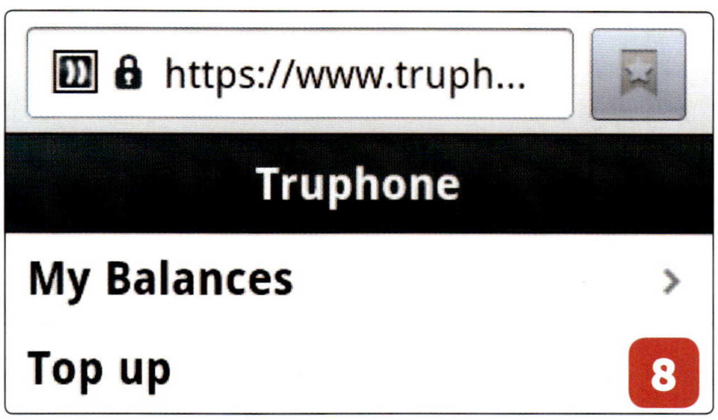

8 Top up credit The app lets you view and top up your Truphone account from your Android device. From the More menu, select My Account. The first time you do this you'll need to enter your mobile phone number for validation. You'll then be able to view your balance and rates, register a credit card and change your password.

Using Vonage

Vonage for Facebook is another app that makes calls over the internet, but with this you call friends from their Facebook profile page. Neither party needs to give out a phone number. It's free and you don't have to subscribe to a VoIP service. Calls are made over 3G or Wi-Fi, whichever connection is available. After installing the app, you sign into your Facebook account and select a friend to call. If you're on the receiving end, the app launches automatically and you can accept or decline.

GET IN TOUCH WITH THE TABLET REVOLUTION

160
PAGES OF ESSENTIAL INFORMATION FOR JUST
£9.99

Available from larger Tesco, Sainsbury's & WH Smith Travel outlets
You can also purchase a digital download now from pcadvisor.co.uk/tabletworld

Social networking

Allow Android to help you stay in touch with family and friends

A big element of having an Android tablet or smartphone is the way that these devices enable you to connect with people using the variety of social-networking sites that are available on the internet. By using such sites as Twitter and Facebook, you can connect with family and friends while you're on the move or lounging on your sofa watching your favourite TV show. However, with an Android device the social aspect can go much further, as you can also use instant-messaging apps or play online games with friends or complete strangers.

1 Seesmic Twitter app Your Android smartphone or tablet will most likely have a pre-installed Twitter app. However, you needn't be limited to just using the one that came with your handheld device as there are plenty of alternatives to choose from at the Android Market. For many hardcore Twitter users, a popular choice is Seesmic, which also works with Facebook. Seesmic does all the important things such as notify you of new messages, lets you share photos and shows thumbnail photos in listings. It will also keep tabs on multiple twitter accounts, making it ideal for power Twitter users.

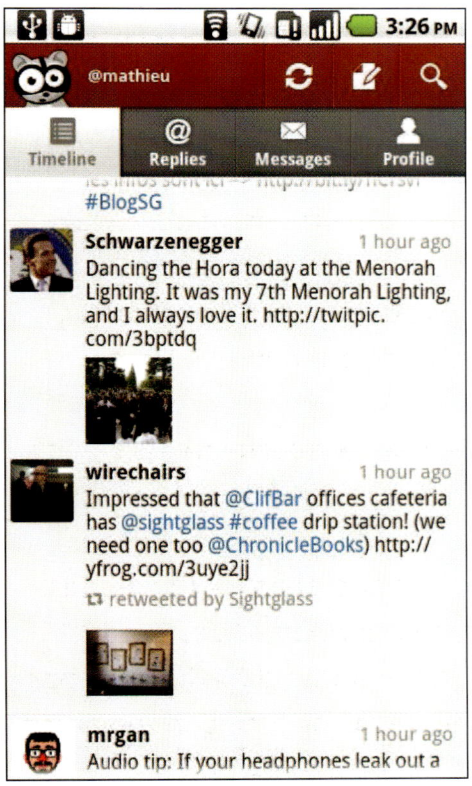

◀ Seesmic is a popular Twitter app for Android

▶ Synchronise your Facebook contacts with the Android contacts app

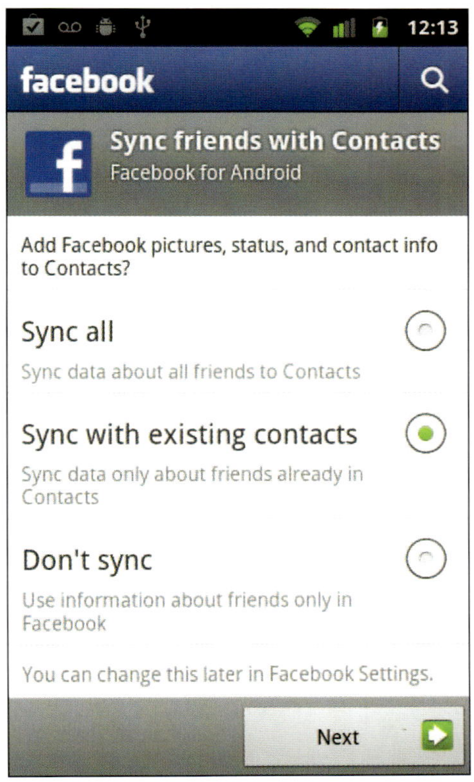

2 Facebook If you'd rather keep your Facebook updates separate from your Twitter client, a pre-installed, dedicated Facebook app may already be on your Android smartphone or tablet. This pre-installed app is more than capable of doing its job. It also has the added advantage of being able to synchronise contact details with the contacts app on the device. The only setting you need to apply is to decide how you want the synchronisation to work.

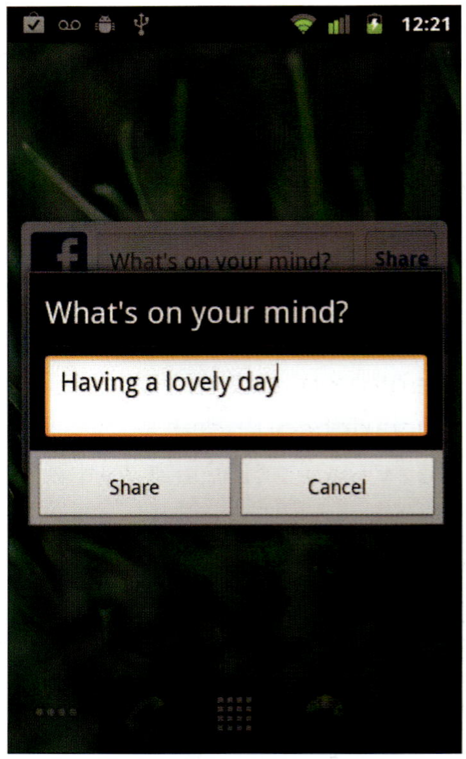

▶ A widget on your home page can make seeing Facebook and Twitter updates a simple task

3 Home page widgets Most Android phone come with a centralised Social Networking app that links to the most common social network sites. However, to improve the functionality of both Twitter and Facebook, you can place widgets on your home screen, which will allow you easy access to your favourite social sites and show updates with new information at regular intervals. Tap and hold on any home screen to see a list of widgets available for your particular Android smartphone or tablet. Tap the one you want and it will be placed on a home screen. Once set up you can easily post direct to Facebook by tapping 'what's on your mind'.

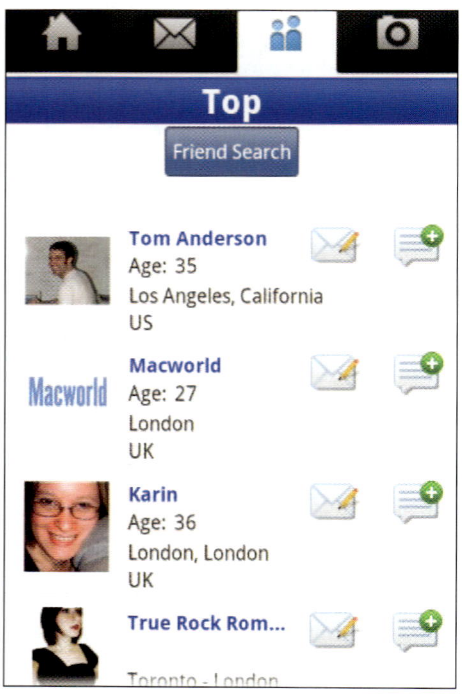

◀ There are apps for most of the popular social networks

4 Other social network sites Let's not forget the other social networks out there. If you are into MySpace, Flickr or LinkedIn, you can find apps for these sites that will run on your Android device. Just hunt around in the Android Market for apps that meet your needs by typing in the name of your favourite social network. >

5 YouTube videos The ability to view YouTube content on your Android device is one of its best features, turning your handheld device into an entertainment gadget. Again, most Android smartphones and tablets will come with a pre-installed YouTube app, so you can enjoy what the video-sharing site has to offer immediately. But Android offers an added feature that is crucial for YouTubers – the ability to upload your videos to the site. In the Gallery, tap the Menu button and choose Share then select your video to upload it.

6 Wordfeud There is another aspect to social networking on the Android: gaming. There are many games available on the Android Market that allow you to play against someone else, whether they're already a friend or a complete stranger. However, we only have space for a couple of examples, so here's our favourite – Wordfeud. This is a Scrabble-like game with

▶ Wordfeud lets you play word games with friends or against randomly selected opponents over 3G or Wi-Fi

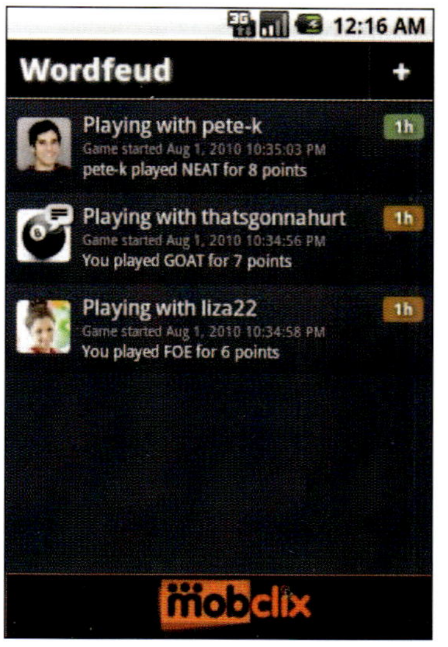

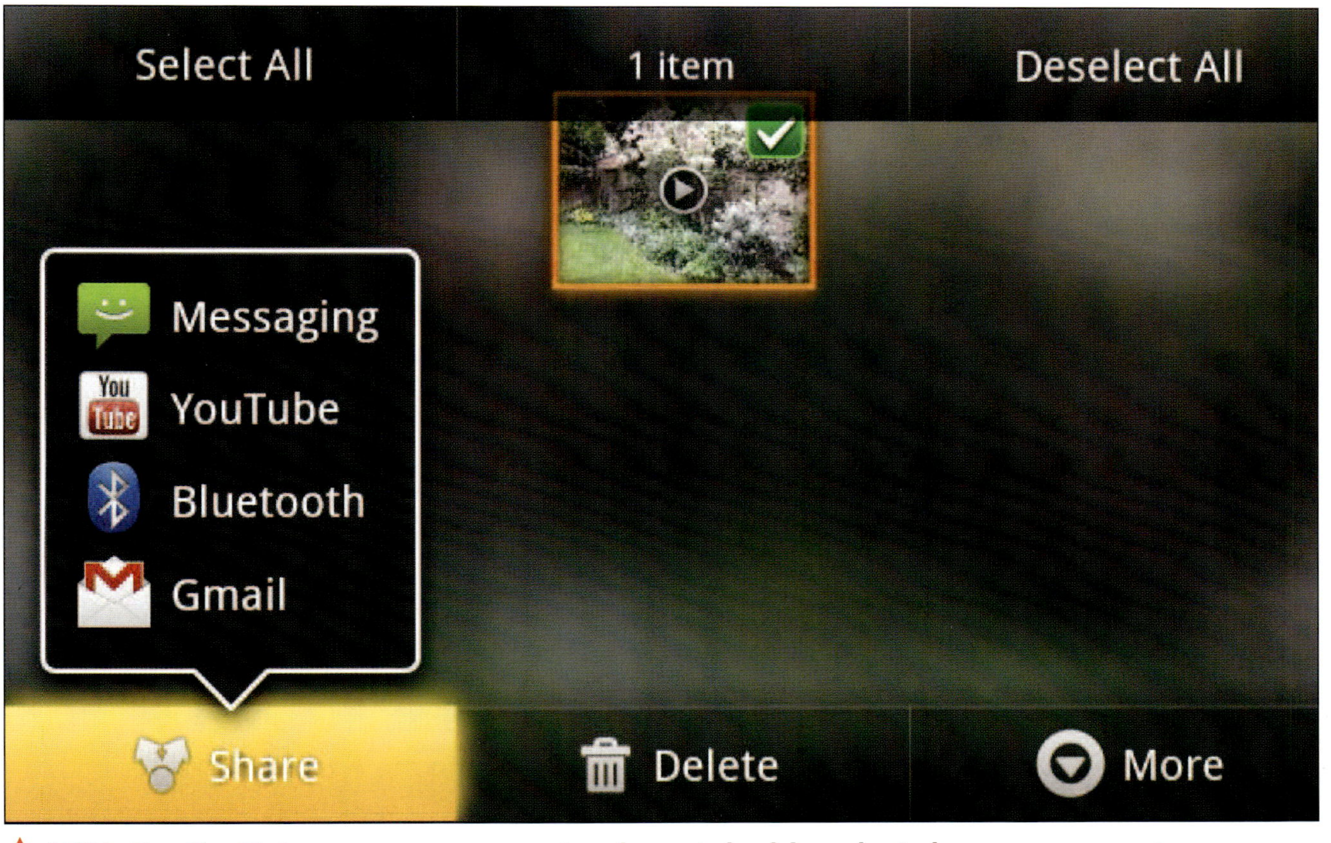

▲ With the YouTube app, you can not only watch videos but share your own too

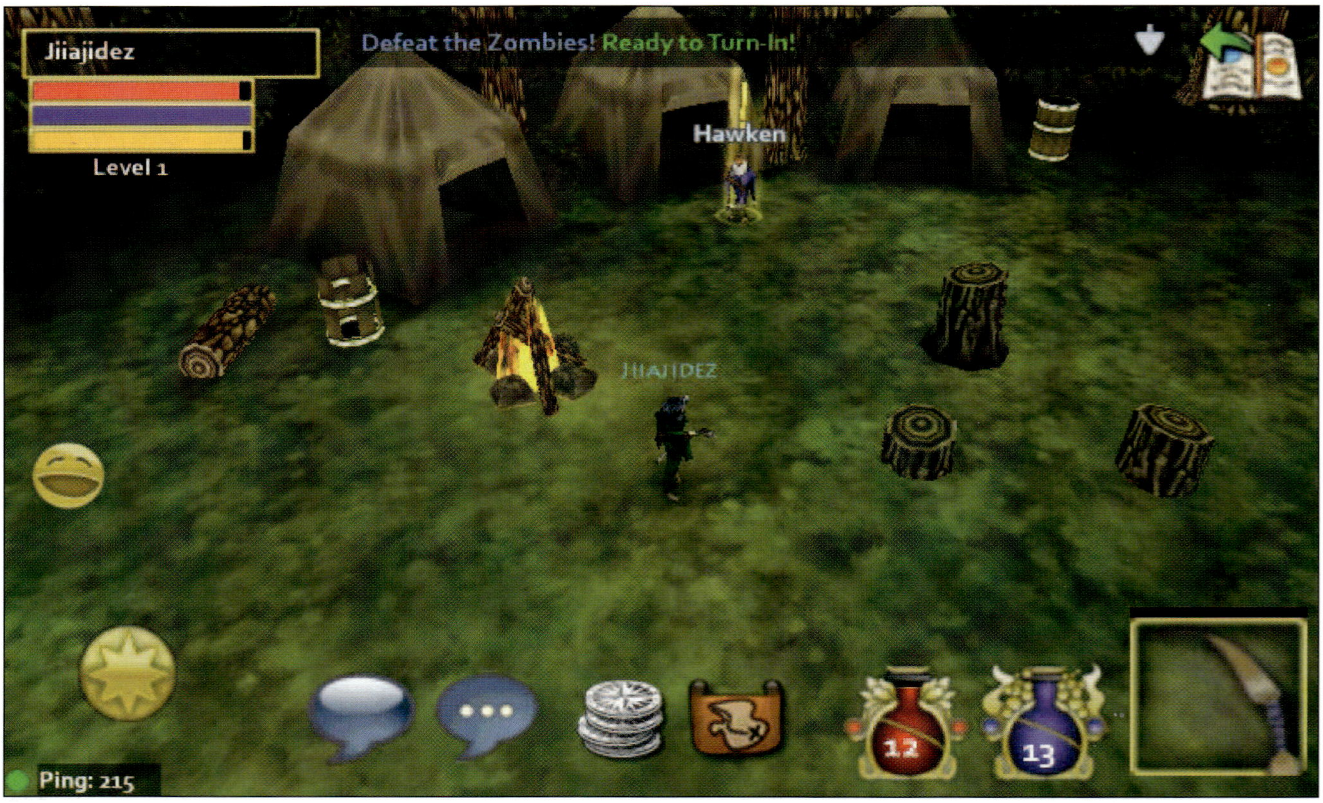

▲ **Pocket Legends is a classic multiplayer role-playing game, which is played online**

a twist – you can play against friends or randomly selected people. You can also play up to 30 games at once. There are free (ad-supported) and paid-for versions.

7 Pocket Legends Our second example is Pocket Legends, which is a multiplayer online game that allows you to take on the role of an avatar and battle in a fantasy world. Free to download, you will find yourself paying in-game for new levels if you get addicted. A big plus is that all the data is stored on a server, meaning that you can log in on to your account with different devices and pick up where you left off.

8 Fring The last app we'll mention here is Fring. This is a multi-purpose chat application that even caters for video calls if your Android smartphone or tablet has a front-facing camera. If you lack one of these, the app can also handle voice calls and instant messaging too, communicating with MSN Messenger, GoogleTalk, AIM and ICQ friends as well as anyone on Fring itself.

▶ **Fring lets you keep in touch with friends in different ways**

Android apps

Chapter 5

Chapter 5

Android apps

One of the main attractions of an Android device, be it smartphone or tablet, is the Android Market. Google's answer to Apple's App Store is home to more than 200,000 apps, and with over one billion app downloads since its launch, it's proved to be a hit with consumers. Best of all, a huge number of these are free, so whether you need an app for work or play, the Android Market has it. >

The Android Market

Google's online store makes it easy to find and buy the apps you need

Despite its excellent operating system, your Android phone is only as useful as the apps installed on it. Whether you're looking to play games, manage media or find new ways to organise your life, apps are the tools that can make it happen.

Android's official app store is the Android Market. While the open nature of Google's platform allows you to download apps from anywhere (several other app download sites exist), the Android Market is the largest collection and offers a secure way to pay through Google Checkout.

THE ANDROID MARKET

To access the Market on your phone or tablet, tap the Market shortcut on the home screen. Once it loads, you'll see a page showcasing the latest featured apps. At the top of the screen is a series of tabs labelled Apps, Games, and possibly another option specific to your network.

Tapping the Apps tab brings up a set of categories to browse. Within each you'll see a list of the most popular programs sorted by whether they're free or paid-for. You can also tap the search icon – the magnifying glass at the top right – to find any application by name or keyword. To learn more about a particular app, tap it to load a description and screenshots provided by the developer, along with ratings and comments from users.

You can't view the Android Market in a web browser, so it's only accessible on an Android device. If you come across a useful app on the developer's website rather than the Market, on the other hand, the website may provide a URL that you can tap (when using an Android device), or a QR code you can scan, to jump to that app's entry in the Android Market.

DOWNLOADING AN APP

When you decide you want an app, touch the Install button at the bottom of its page in the Market. The vast majority of apps in

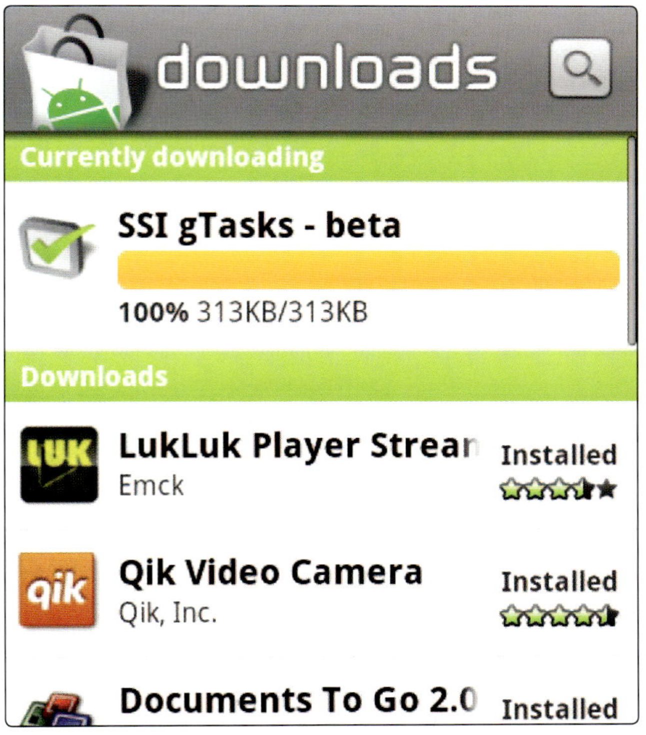

▲ As you download an app, the Downloads screen will show progress

How to use QR codes

You'll notice square, barcode-like boxes scattered throughout this chapter. If you've not encountered them before, all you need to know is that they are quick links. Point your smartphone or tablet's camera at a box and it will scan the graphic and show you a web link where you can find out further information about the product. In the case of the app reviews we feature, the QR codes take you to the App Market. The code above, for example, takes you to a free QR code reader called QuickMark (www.quickmark.cn).

Some handset makers install a QR code reader on the device, so you have everything you need straight out of the box. Launch this and point the camera at the QR code. You may not even need to press the camera icon to take the shot – some apps produce a haptic 'shudder' to indicate recognition. Next, press to see the web address the code relates to, then click on the browser icon to continue to the site.

the Market are perfectly safe. Just be sure you've looked over an app's ratings and comments to get an idea of its reputation, then use your judgement.

With free apps, the download will begin as soon as you tap OK. With paid apps, you'll first be taken to a Google Checkout screen to enter your credit card information. You'll have to input your payment details only once; they'll be securely stored for future transactions. A message will pop up in your notification panel once an app has finished installing.

UPDATING AND UNINSTALLING

Many apps receive regular updates from their developers. The Android Market will notify you by placing a Market icon with an 'Updates available' message in your notification panel. Follow the prompts to download and install the update for free.

To manually check for updates, press the Menu key while in the Market, then select Downloads. Any app that's been updated appears at the top with a label.

If you want to uninstall an app, go to the Market and access the Downloads menu. Touch any app in the list and you'll get an option to uninstall it. The Android Market will refund your money on any paid app you uninstall within 24 hours, provided you haven't had it before.

Your Android device has its own built-in app manager, too. Tap the Menu key while on your home screen, then select Settings, Applications, Manage applications. You'll find a list of all the programs installed on your device. Tapping on any app lets you see detailed information about its system resource usage and will also give you the option to uninstall it.

Music

Shazam

★★★★☆ FREE

Shazam is one of those slightly oddball ideas that just works. It's a free music-recognition service that requires only a few seconds' burst of a track in order to pinpoint the artist and title.

Unlike sticking a CD into your laptop and having the track listing and album art pop up in Windows Media Player or iTunes, Shazam doesn't rely on existing info, but uses rhythm and audio characteristics to identify what's playing. So if you're listening to the FM radio on your Android phone, you don't have to wait for the DJ to announce what they've played – Shazam will tell you first.

NAME THAT TUNE

When we first heard about this system some years ago, we were sceptical. But then we had the opportunity to try it out in the high-pressure environment of a pub quiz and we found it came up trumps every time. Shazam even correctly identified live music tracks and concert footage featuring cover versions. Surely some kind of voodoo is at play here?

Another cool element is tagging. You can tag a track and share it with friends or find out who else is tagging songs. A live tag stream can be displayed within Shazam. If you buy the Encore version you can tag as many tracks as you like and pull other people's tagged tracks in to your playlists. The free version limits you to tagging five tunes a month, which is only a limitation if you get a taste for it.

The makers are also working to link Shazam with other ways of experiencing music. Tagging an artist causes information about their upcoming gigs and music releases to be pushed in your direction. And now that Android supports PayPal and mobile payments, the ability to buy concert tickets for your favourite artists will also come into its own.

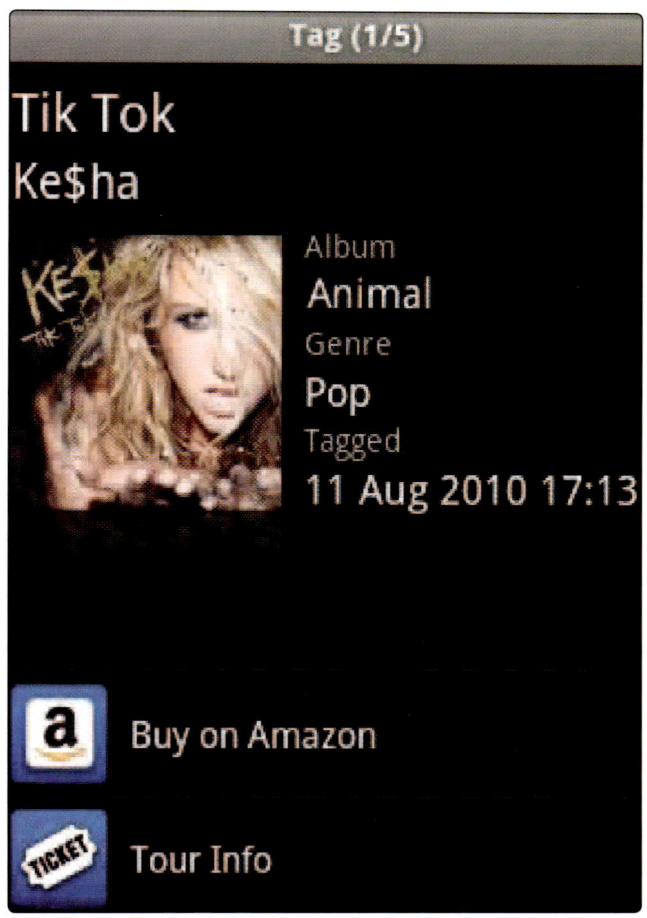

Spotify

★★★★½ FREE

Spotify has quickly become one of the most popular music-streaming services around. It comes in a free, ad-supported version, one free of advertising interruptions, and a mobile version that allows you to download playlists from the desktop application and play them on your smartphone in offline mode. The latter service costs £9.99 a month, so you'd need to be a fairly committed music fan and make extensive use of its library.

Spotify also suggests that this is a useful option if you're travelling abroad and want to be able to access your favourite Spotify albums: just download them to your Android device before you go. A similar principle to Napster's streaming service applies to accessing your stored Spotify tracks: you have a full month to listen to a downloaded track before the service checks that your subscription is still active. You can also synchronise your library with up to three PCs or Macs.

STREAMING HOT

Sensibly, playlists and albums download only when you have a Wi-Fi connection, saving your 3G data allowance and battery life. Music can be streamed over a cell network connection as well as Wi-Fi.

Another advantage of signing up for a Spotify subscription is that you can access new albums before they become available to users of the free service. As with Shazam, sharing is a big element; you can create a playlist and share it on Facebook or Twitter, via email and so on.

Spotify's music catalogue is broader than some, so you're not stuck with Katy Perry and Take That, but can rediscover alternative gems from your youth. The only real issue we have with the Android version is that support for hardware is more limited that we'd have expected.

Of the eight Android devices we had to hand when we came to try out Spotify for Android, only three – the LG GW620 and the Sony Ericsson Xperia models – proved to be compatible with it. As of April 2011, 28 Android devices were supported in total.

Last.fm

FREE

Music geeks and Android lovers unite! Last.fm is an across-the-board great application. Boasting 'the world's largest online music catalogue', the service itself probably needs no introduction; it's already used by more than 40 million music lovers worldwide. The Android app brings it within reach of even more.

If you already have a Last.fm account, you can simply sign in to jump to the service's homepage. If you don't yet have one, setting up an account takes only a minute within the app. The homepage has tabs for Artist, Tag and User along with a search bar. We tried a search for Pixies, and almost immediately Frank Black's voice started singing from the speakers.

STALK THE STARS

When Last.fm plays a song by an artist who's currently touring, the upper right corner of the album artwork displays a banner that says 'On Tour'. Clicking this leads to an artist bio, a 'similar artists' tab, tags, fans and events. The information on events includes a listing of all nearby shows that this artist is playing along with their dates and venues.

The Radio tab holds all the stations that you've recently listened to, as well as a list of recommended artists and popular artists in your local area. The Profile tab will show your top artists, top albums, top tracks, recently played music, events, friends and tags.

We enjoyed playing around with this app, which performed nearly flawlessly, and kept finding pleasant surprises in each new feature. For instance, Last.fm has background streaming, so you can listen continuously while using other features of your smartphone, very handy if you need to quickly send an email. We were also pleased to find that you can purchase songs direct from the Amazon music store from within the app.

Though we did miss a pause button, we could probably have kept Last.fm running all day – if only the speakers on our Android smartphone weren't so tinny.

SoundHound

FREE

Few things are as annoying as hearing a song on the radio or the TV and not being able to recall the track's title or the artist. And SoundHound aims to answer these nagging questions.

Although similar to Shazam, SoundHound packs in a few extra tools. Using the Sound2Sound search engine to accurately identify music, SoundHound can listen to a song being played on the radio and recognise it, like Shazam. But SoundHound can also identify songs that you sing or hum. In addition, you can also just speak a song's title or an artist's name into your device's built-in mic and SoundHound will find it.

No internet connection? No problem – your search will be saved and marked as pending under the history tab until you connect with a network again. SoundHound lets you bookmark your searches and share the songs you find through Twitter, Facebook, or email.

Once SoundHound has identified a song, it brings up a plethora of information. The song title and artist name appears at the top of the screen, along with a 30-second preview and a link to download it through Amazon. Below that, you'll find several links to YouTube, where you can watch music videos. SoundHound's results page also features a tab that will launch a Google search for the song's lyrics, which is a great way to settle arguments. If you're still hungry for more info, there's even artist and album info tabs, which bring up album reviews, photos, top songs, a discography, similar artists, and even a biography.

SIMPLE AND ATTRACTIVE

SoundHound has a simple and attractive interface, making the app easy to use right out of the box. The accuracy with which it identifies songs is impressive. Even with relatively obscure songs, SoundHound nailed it every time.

More than just a way to identify songs, SoundHound puts a wealth of musical information at your fingertips.

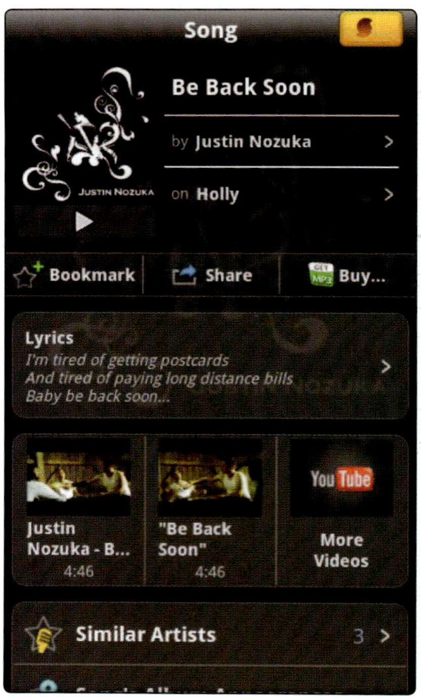

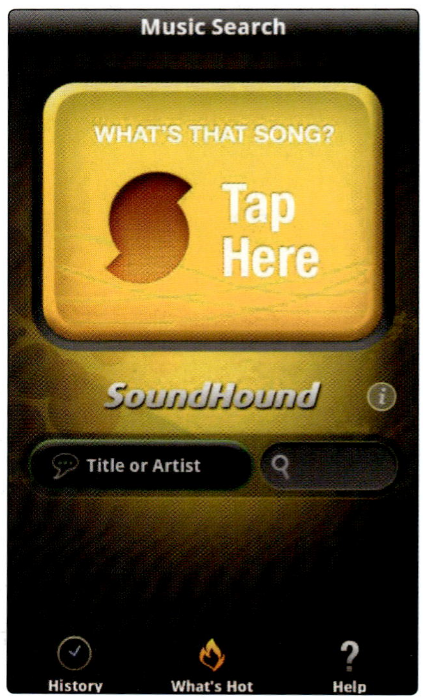

Cherry Rplayer

★★★★☆ FREE

You don't have to be a jet-setter to groove to Santa Monica's KCRW in the morning, bop with BBC Radio 1 through the day and bounce to J-pop all night long on Colombia's TokyoNext radio. You just need Cherry Rplayer. This app can play Shoutcast, Icecast, AAC, MP3, M3U, PLS, AACP and other internet radio streams, and will download track, artist and song lyrics on demand.

Despite the odd name, it's far superior to its closest rival, StreamFurious. Four tabs help music fans navigate through the options, which include the ability to drill down through radio stations by city and search or browse through stations promoted via Shoutcast or Icecast. When you find a station you like, click the heart icon near the foot of the screen to add it to your Favorites, which appear under a tab of that name. If you forget a station's name, you can view a history of streams you've visited before.

It's not the player's fault, but the packed US radio market isn't as well represented as we would have hoped in the US Radio tab, and the listings are cluttered with AM talk radio stations. If you know of a station and it isn't listed under its city, try the search function on the World/Live tab; you can usually find it there by its call sign.

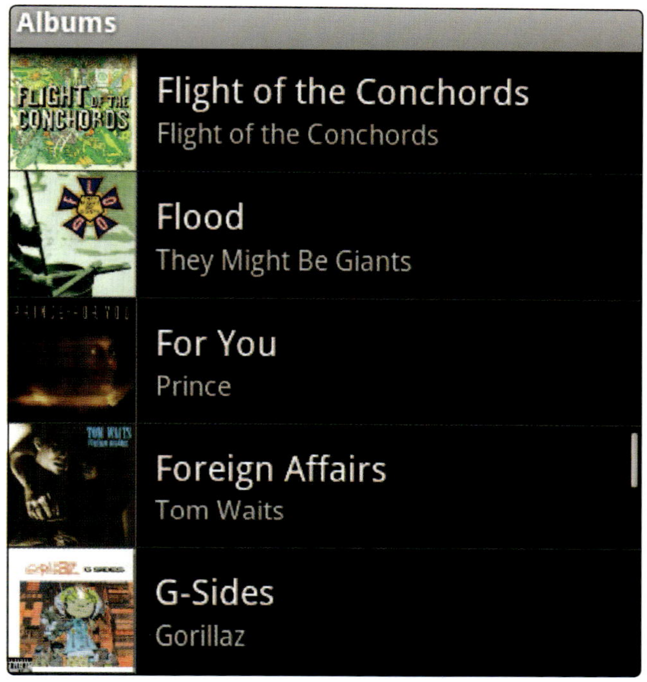

We7 Radio Plus

★★★½☆ FREE

We7 is a rival service to Spotify, enabling desktop users to stream from more than 6.5 million tracks for free (like Spotify, Android users have to pay for premium accounts, however).

We7 also has this rather nifty free radio app. The idea is that you 'charge' up your phone with music as you charge it up with power. You can choose music by track, artists, or theme and the We7 app creates personalised radio stations based upon those choices. It's an interesting way to listen to your favourite type of music, and while you don't get the same level of control as you do on the desktop application, it's a good way to discover new music. Worth checking out.

NPR News

FREE

The radio isn't just about music, it can also be a good source for keeping up with current affairs when you're on the move. The NPR News app taps into the wealth of content offered by the National Public Radio media organisation, which creates and distributes news, information and music programming to a network of 900 independent radio stations in the US. If you have already come across the NPR website in your trawls for news stories, then this app will be familiar territory for you, just in a slightly more convenient package.

The prominent feature of NPR News is, surprisingly enough, news. The main screen presents multiple news categories that allow you to browse the current news, view news photos, and listen to audio clips from the related broadcast, as well as the hourly newscast. If you'd like to tune into your local news, you can also find the live stream for any public radio station in the country that supports it and even set a list of favourite stations for quick access.

If you're a fan of the regular programs that NPR broadcasts, this app has got you covered. Much like the online NPR experience, the NPR News app gives full access to the broadcaster's podcast archive; you can listen to podcasts individually or add them to a playlist that can handle all of the audio content in the app.

SPREAD THE NEWS

What really sets NPR News apart from other news and radio apps is its sharing abilities. Once configured, you can share any news story that has caught your eye with friends using email, Twitter, or Facebook with a single click.

Simply put, if you like NPR and find yourself with a craving for great public radio on the go, albeit with a US slant, this app is a great solution. There are drawbacks in lack of textual local news and push notification of breaking stories. And since it's a free app, you'll have to contend with ads. Still, that's a small trade-off to make for a great app.

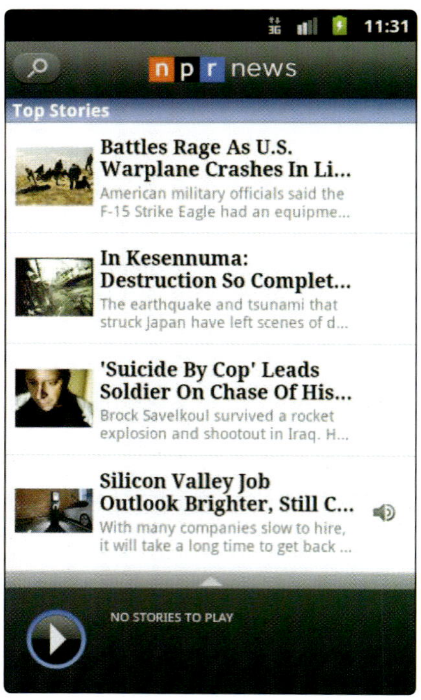

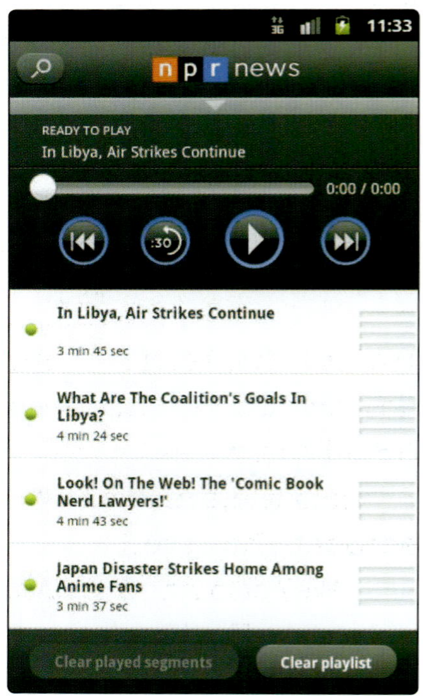

TV and movies

IMDb

FREE

The Internet Movie Database (IMDb) has rightly become a must-visit web destination for film buffs keen to gen up on their movie knowledge. And this Android app brings the vast film resource to your fingertips.

The IMDb app is divided into Movies, Television and People sections. The top portion of the screen fills with images of the most-viewed IMDb content, which you can browse through by scrolling horizontally. Below that, the material available varies from category to category.

In the Movies section, box-office results, the top 250 movies, the bottom 100 films, popular movies by genre, and other topics. The Television section lists recaps, popular shows and the latest TV news. In the People section you can see a list of Hollywood stars that have a birthday that day and the latest celebrity news.

Clicking on a movie or TV show brings up the same sort of information you expect to see on the IMDb website, such as trailers, ratings, the release date, a plot summary, the cast, and other details like trivia and quotes. Clicking on a person's profile displays their bio and filmography.

The formatting of IMDb is attractive, and it is easy to browse and read. The app also has links to the host website, as well as to Amazon for DVD or Blu-ray purchases. By default, this is set to the US, but you can easily change the URLs by going to the settings menu and choosing your preferred country. The only niggle is that to start a search you are forced to return to the menu instead of having a search bar at the top of the screen.

NO PLACE LIKE HOME

IMDb says it has details of more than 1.5 million films, cross-referenced with 3.5 million actors, directors, producers, cinematographers and other key players. As well as providing completists with a list of lesser-known parts played by Clint Eastwood or James Coburn, for example, it helps you decide which films are worth watching. You can also find out which of the latest releases are worth seeing thanks to its links to online reviews, while a tie in with Amazon allows you to order the movie for viewing at home. All in all, the IMDb app is an excellent freebie.

Movies

FREE

We've tried a handful of movie-listing apps, and generally they range from the comically bad to the merely competent. This app from Flixster, simply titled Movies, puts all the other apps to shame. Attractively designed, it has a smart interface that allows the user to discover what flicks are playing, and it includes plenty of other neat features, too.

The browsable categories include Box Office, Theaters, Upcoming, DVD, and My Movies. The straightforward Box Office listings allow you to browse by movie title. You see each movie's score on the popular review website Rotten Tomatoes, the main actors, the rating, the length of the film, and how much money the film has grossed so far. If you click on any particular title, you get even more information, such as a video link to the trailer, photos, and an expanded cast list. On the Theater tab you can search for cinemas in your area either by name or by distance from your post code within a 25-mile range.

WHAT'S ON

The Upcoming tab lets you keep track of movies coming out soon. Both this tab and the one for new DVD releases are as easy to browse as the Box Office listings tab is, and include similar information.

You can personalise the app, with lists of your favourite movies, reviews, pictures, and the like. It can also connect to and work with websites such as Facebook, Flixster, and Netflix.

The app is not without its flaws. Occasionally, a screen is slow to load. Still, overall Movies is a tremendous app that does a lot of things right.

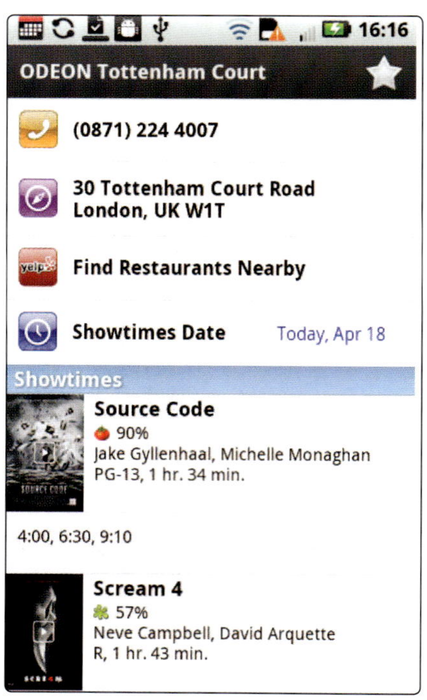

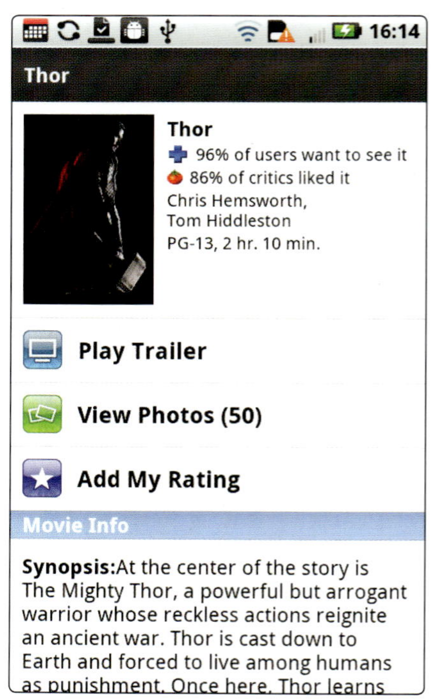

Photography and art

PicSay

FREE

If you're the sort of person who sends wacky greetings cards, you may well find PicSay appealing. It lets you 'say it within a picture' by adding a speech bubble, a caption or fun effects. A slider at the top of the screen lets you increase or reduce an effect such as Distort or Pixelize.

Having adjusted your image, you can add titles and speech balloons. Stickers include Hats & Helmets, Hair and so on. A Pro edition (available from the Android Market for £2.63) offers font options and more than 400 stickers.

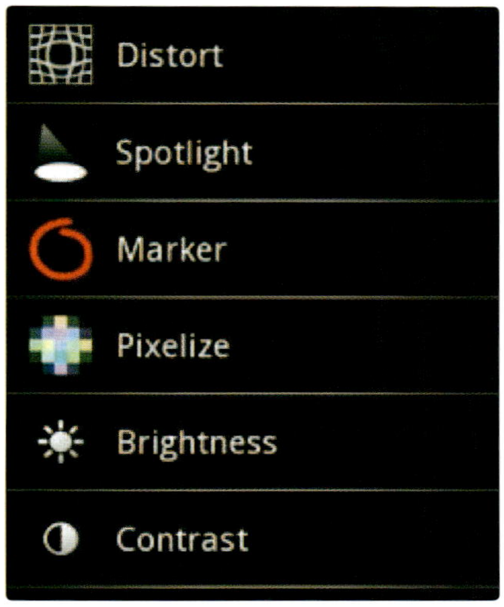

PhotoFunia

FREE

PhotoFunia is another neat little whimsy of an app that lets you get all arty with your photos. Rather than installing the effects as software on your Android device, it runs them online. To get started, you choose an effect you want to apply and then browse to a suitable source image stored on your phone or its SD card. If there's nothing suitable in your Android Gallery, you can take a new shot. Of note is the fact that you can use both front and rear cameras on your device. We tried this with the Sphinx effect and a shot of Tigger, but the resulting effect – which makes use of built-in face detection – was so subtle we almost missed it. The Mona Lisa in the art gallery was far more effective and we also liked adding our subject to a jigsaw puzzle.

FxCamera

FREE

FxCamera needs little explanation. It's a free (and discreetly ad-supported) app for your Android device that lets you apply a range of zany and arty effects on to your snaps. There's a broad selection of effects to choose from, so you're bound to find something that appeals. The biggest limitation is that you can customise photos only as you take them; there's no facility to load a picture already stored on your device and add effects to it after the fact.

Among the filters included, FishEye and Polandroid offer subtle artiness, making your picture appear to have been shot with an extreme wide-angle lens or a traditional instant film camera. Other effects are more radical. You've probably got a fair idea what's going to happen if you choose the AndyWarholizer option. We got mixed results with this Pop Art effect, but had lots of fun playing. Images with hard, distinct outlines worked well, while fuzzy edges were less successful.

For out and out weirdness the SymmetriCam option wins hands down. You position the subject in the left half of the screen (held horizontally). Click the Shot button and you'll get a mirror of it on the right.

This app has had a few issues with Defy handsets, but for a freebie, FxCamera is good, straightforward fun.

ToonPaint

★★★★☆ £1.22

If you've ever wanted to create a cartoon-style image of yourself but don't have the artistic skills to make it happen, you should check out ToonPaint from Toon-FX. Choose an existing photo or take a new one with the iPhone's camera, and ToonPaint then produces a "MagiSketch" – a cartoon-style sketch of your image.

You can then adjust the resulting sketch using sliders at the bottom of the screen. The edges slider determines the amount of edge hardness while the black and gray sliders determine the amount of black or gray in your sketch. You can also toggle between hard and soft sliders for a more soft- or hard-edged look.

An advanced tab offers even more variables for you to tweak. There's coherence, which determines just how closely the sketch follows the lines in your source image. Edge width and edge length alters the lines in your sketch. A soften button will give a smoother look to your sketch.

Once you have your sketch the way you like it, it's time to add colour to complete the cartoon-look. Tapping one of the four swatches at the bottom of the screen selects that colour; a double tap lets you change it. There is also the option to select colours via a rainbow picker and you can use an eyedropper tool to select a colour from the canvas or the source image.

A slider lets you adjust the size of the brush. When you zoom in, the size of the brush scales down automatically and then scales back up when you zoom back out, which is a neat touch.

An undo button will undo or redo the last stroke you made; you can also opt to erase all the paint at once. Unfortunately, you can undo only one step, so if the mistake was two stages back, you'll just have to paint over it in white – think of it as an eraser. After you're done with your masterpiece, you can save it to your camera roll as just the sketch or the sketch and colour.

Not only do the images look awesome, but creating them is both easy and fun to do.

SketchBook Express

★★★★☆ **FREE**

Do you like to draw, but are too self-conscious to carry a sketchbook around with you? Maybe you think you're just too busy or not talented enough for that stuff. With the SketchBook Express (free, or 62p for SketchBook Mobile with advanced features), you can turn your downtime into doodle time.

It has a slick interface that pops up when you need it and stays out of your way when you don't. One button-press brings up an icon-based menu with various brush, pen, pencil, eraser, smudge, airbrush, and bucket-fill options. The app also has multiple levels of undo and redo. To change colours, touch the square icon at the top of the screen and select your colour from the RGB colour wheel. You can even use an eyedropper colour picker to match colours.

One of the best features is the ability to add new layers to your drawing (top-right icon). The new layer can be a photo from the Camera or Gallery app, or it can be another drawing. Although a small screen does impose some limitations, the app has pinch-and-zoom multitouch capability, so you can zoom into an area for detailed work and then zoom out for the big picture (up to 1024 x 768 pixels).

SketchBook lacks a cut/paste function, something that would be very useful. Similarly, you can't fill an area with a texture, and there's no way to insert text or text-art into a picture.

The app lets you save your drawing as a PNG image. However, it doesn't let you choose a file name – it just names the drawing "sketch" followed by a string of numbers. The paid-for version lets you save in JPEG, PNG, or PSD formats.

It would be nice to be able to share drawings via email or Facebook, directly from the app, but that's not an option. You must save the drawing first (Menu, New, Export), and then open another app to share it. Aside from these small criticisms, SketchBook Express is a fun, easy way to explore your creativity.

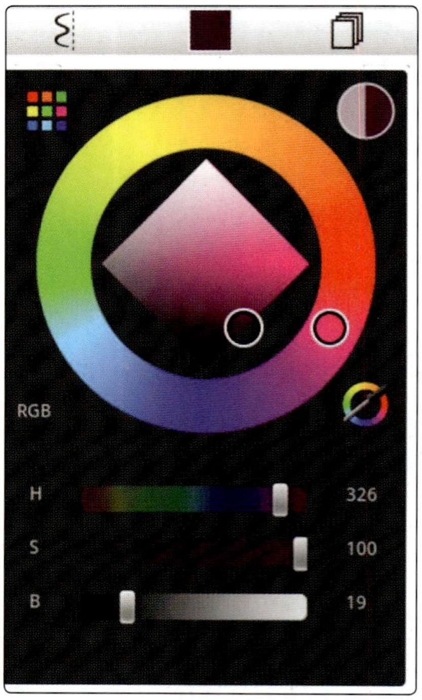

Reference

Wikidroid

★★★★☆ FREE

Want access to the world's most popular encyclopedia, wherever you are? Then you need Wikidroid. You'll get full Wikipedia content on your Android smartphone, including live links and graphics.

The app is in essence a front end to the popular online encyclopedia. Do a search, and the Android app grabs the relevant information from Wikipedia, formats it so it displays nicely on your Android phone, and then delivers it to you. You get all of Wikipedia's content, including graphics and live links.

When you do searches, Wikidroid suggests potential matches, shortening your searching time. You can even do voice searches. When you tap the search option, a small button of a microphone appears next to the search box, in the same way it does when you search Google on your Android phone. Tap the button, speak your search, and it goes to work. The voice search uses the same engine as the rest of Android's voice-searching, so it works in the same way.

SHARE BOOKMARKS

There's more. You can create bookmarks and share them with others, and also ask to see a random page. In addition, the app includes many of the Android tools available when you browse to web pages, so you can select text and copy it to the Android clipboard, or share the page with others via email, SMS text messaging, Bluetooth, and social-networking apps such as Facebook. You can also change what language to use with Wikipedia. And you can zoom in and out with the same tools as you can on other Android apps.

If you want to be able to save pages to your Android phone so you can view them offline, you'll need to buy the Wikidroid Plus version for £1.24.

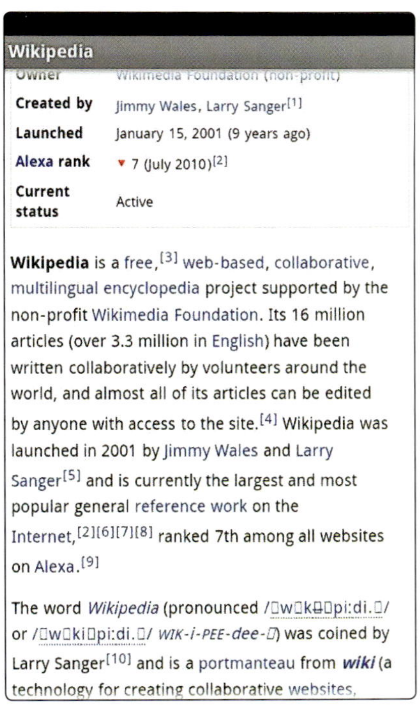

Britannica Encyclopedia

★★★☆☆ **£12.43**

When it comes to fact-finding and pursuing points of knowledge, it's all very well having the internet at your fingertips on your smartphone – but that counts for nothing when you're not online. That's one of the main reasons for keeping an offline resource such as the Britannica Encyclopedia on your device. The other mooted benefit is that – unlike Wikipedia – there ought to be a good chance that entries are factually correct and not the result of a misinformed contribution or even malicious misinformation.

LIMITED DESCRIPTIONS

We've looked at the PC version of Encyclopedia Britannica before, and this app carries similar limitations. There may be more than 35,000 articles here, but you'll still find that most subjects only receive a cursory description. 'Camera', the picture-taking device with a long history, is described in 184 words. 'Earth', our world, gets more than just 'mostly harmless', but at 264 words it still feels a little short for a resumé of the planet. But there is a small illustration, in this case a pie-slice through the crust and core. The app lists 2,700 included images, so only about one in ten entries are given these basic illustrations. For any entry that you alight upon, you can send it in its (brief) entirety to a friend by email with the simple tap of a button located at the top of the screen. You can save any page entry as a Favorite here, too. Meanwhile, at the bottom of the app's home screen is an 'On This Day' button, which calls up a list of historical events for that day. Getting even more esoteric, you can give your phone a little shake to receive a random entry.

At £12.43, it's relatively expensive for an app, but may prove useful for pulling up some outline knowledge on a wide range of subjects when you're missing an Internet connection. If only its database was more comprehensive then we might find this app indispensable to have around on our travels.

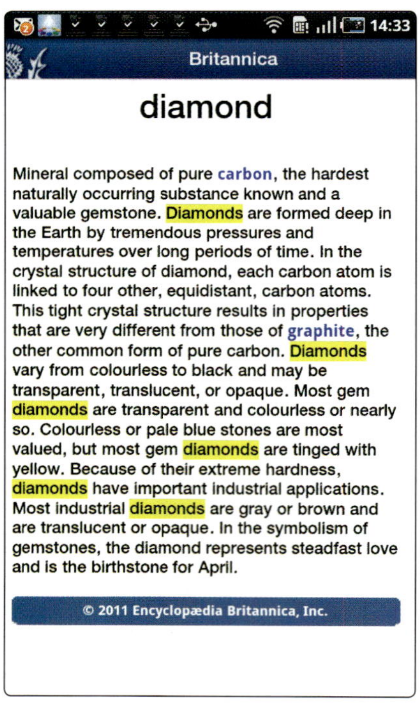

Books and media sharing

2Player DLNA

★★★½ FREE

Digital Living Network Alliance is a clunky acronym that's worth looking out for when choosing consumer electronics to share media across your home Wi-Fi setup. DNLA promises interoperability between devices, so you can mix and match, say, Sony, Philips and Toshiba laptops, flat-screen TVs and media hubs. DNLA apps such as this one allow you to push media from device to device. Some Android phones have a version preloaded; otherwise this edition rates highly.

INS AND OUTS

The DLNA app allows you to control how you share the kind of content you might want to enjoy on such devices. You can share photos, music and video (singly or all three) both to and from your Android handset, allowing you to stream albums to a set of wireless speakers, for example.

A helpful warning when you fire up the DLNA software checks whether you want to leave the Wi-Fi radio function switched on or turn it off for the moment.

The simplicity of setup is one of the strengths of the DLNA app. Four tiles allow you to copy media to and from the server and the phone and to toggle the sharing function on and off. Clicking on an option brings up a screen offering a choice of available media servers. If you've bought music on your Android device, you can stream this to a suitably connected speaker. Clicking on the Play button lets you either access media server content or play items stored on the Android device, using the DLNA app like a regular media player. However, our biggest gripe was that we found the software slow at accessing content, even when it was stored locally.

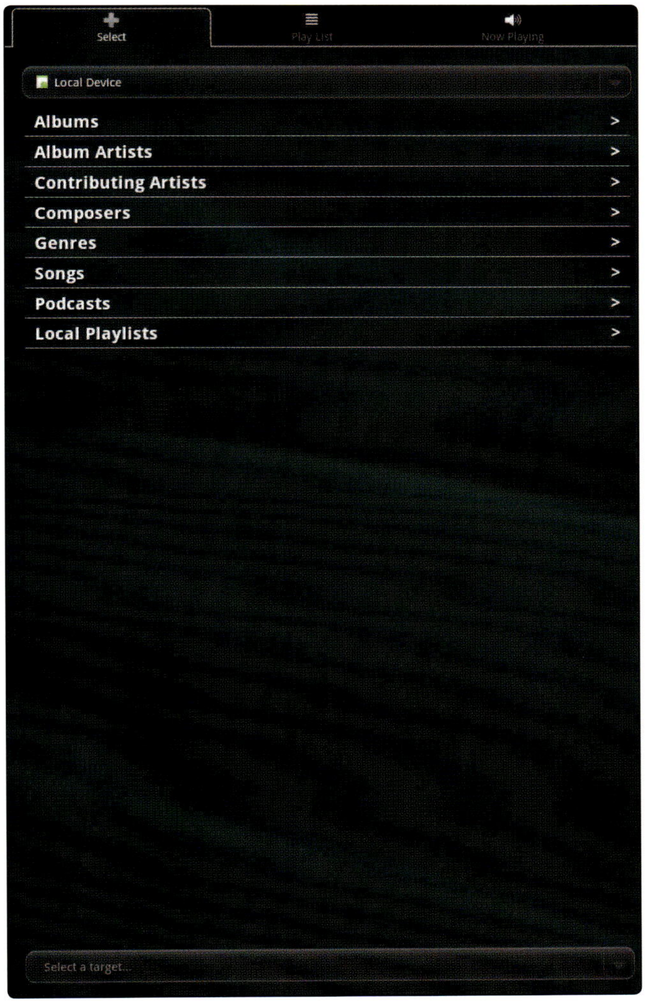

Dictionary.com

FREE

Even the best wordsmiths have their off days when the 'mot juste' just won't come to mind. Dictionary.com pairs a 375,000-word database with the Thesaurus.com phrase finder in a free app that installs almost instantly from the Android Market.

Definitions, synonyms and antonyms are all provided, along with a pronunciation guide, and there's even a Word of the Day.

Though the principle of this app is sound, we came across a few issues that betray its US provenance. It does claim to be localised for the UK – indeed Dictionary.com asks your permission to log your geographical location – but its entry for 'aluminium' gave us a phonetic pronunciation while listing the word as an alternative to 'aluminum'.

Amazon Kindle

FREE

Reading an eBook is considerably more practical on a 7in or 10in tablet than a 3.5in smartphone, but whatever the size of your device it's worth downloading this app. After setting up a free account, you even get enough credit to buy your first book at no cost.

If you already have an Amazon account, you can log in using this and will be able to download any books you've bought previously. An on-screen status message tells you how recently content was synced from Amazon, so you don't need to bother logging on just in case.

Amazon claims more than 620,000 titles are available for viewing through Kindle, though the full complement is not available outside the US. The first chapter of each book can be downloaded before you decide to buy it.

If you can read websites and spend hours Facebook-messaging on your mobile device, you shouldn't find reading a gripping novel too much of a stretch.

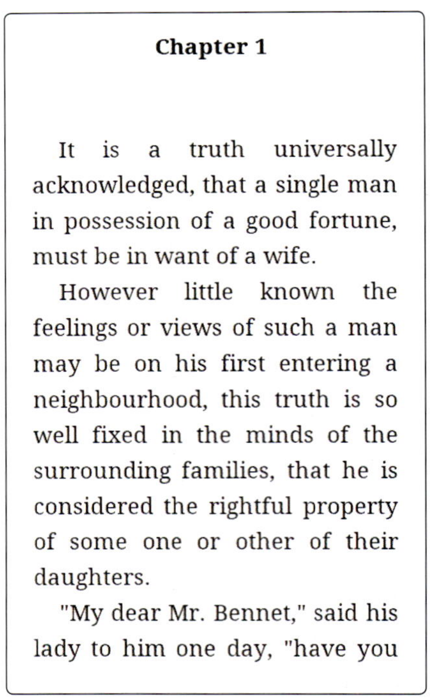
Chapter 1

It is a truth universally acknowledged, that a single man in possession of a good fortune, must be in want of a wife.

However little known the feelings or views of such a man may be on his first entering a neighbourhood, this truth is so well fixed in the minds of the surrounding families, that he is considered the rightful property of some one or other of their daughters.

"My dear Mr. Bennet," said his lady to him one day, "have you

Productivity

ThinkFree Office Mobile

★★★★★ £9.34

One of the frustrating things about Android is its weak support of Microsoft Office files. ThinkFree Office Mobile aims to remedy this by letting you view, edit and create Office documents. In addition, 1GB of cloud storage is provided, which integrates with ThinkFree's web-based office app for desktop browsers.

As a document viewer, it performs well, displaying almost all types of documents. Unfortunately, when editing Word files, you can apply only basic formatting. Support for Excel files is also a big disappointment. In our tests, several timesheet-style spreadsheets wouldn't open. Those with basic formatting will open, though the features are limited. PowerPoint support is much better, and ThinkFree Office Mobile is one of the few mobile apps that can produce a presentation with images.

ONLINE STORAGE

The cloud storage and document collaboration feature is a nice touch. To upload or share a file, you must first register an account at ThinkFree Online. You can do this in the app or in a desktop browser; afterwards, you log in through the app. Within the app, you'll see an integrated file browser with tabs to toggle between views of your device's SD card and your ThinkFree online storage.

To share a file on your SD card, just tap and hold the file until the dialog box pops up, and then select Upload. Select or create a destination folder, click Choose and the file will upload. Toggle to the Online tab, select and hold the file, and choose the Share option. Enter an email address and a message, and then click Share. Now you and the recipient can collaborate on the same file.

Although ThinkFree has some nice features, as yet it feels a little half-baked. We recommend trying the free viewer first and then looking at the desktop browser version of ThinkFree Online.

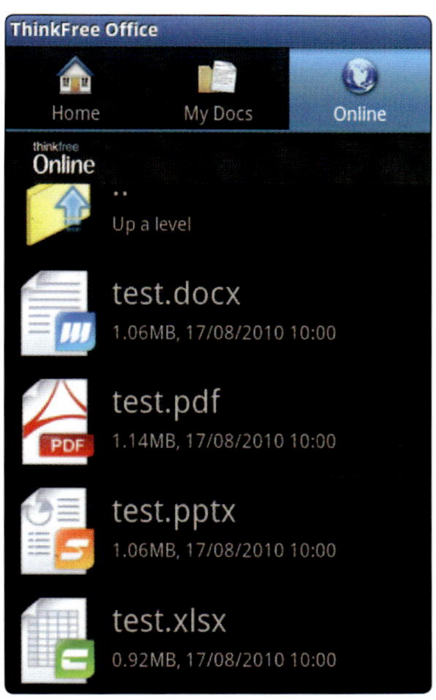

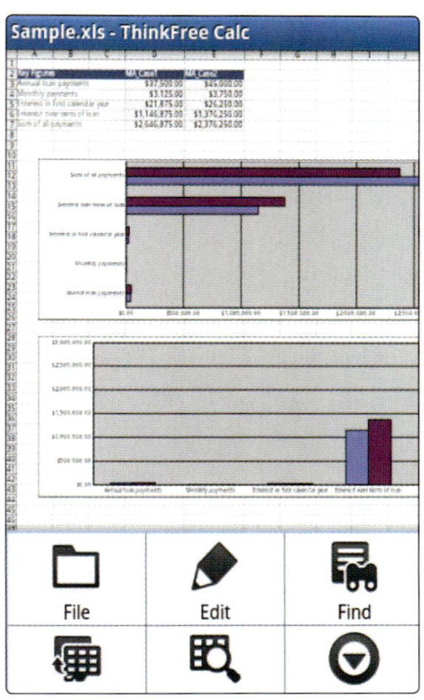

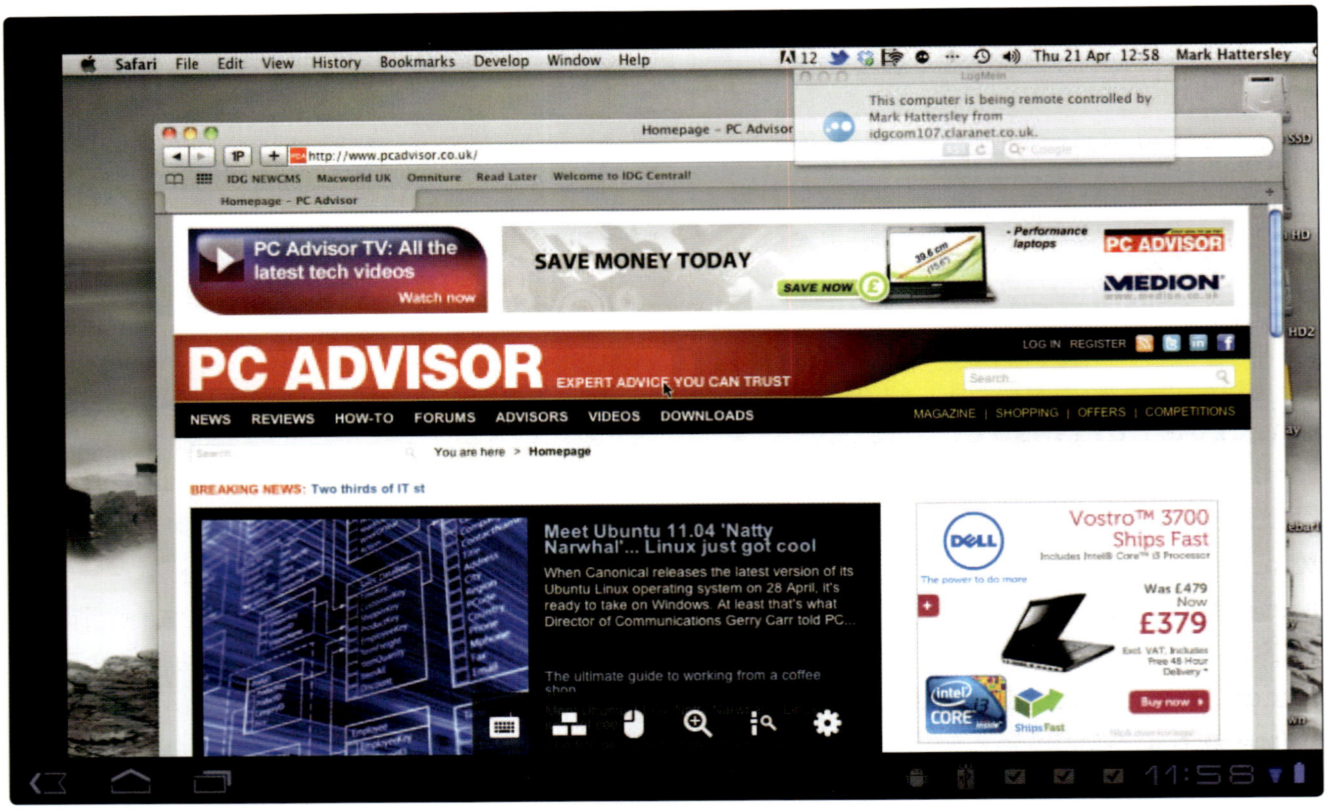

LogMeIn Ignition

★★★★★ £18.68

Remote access software is all well and good, but the time you really need it is when you are away from any computer. Enter LogMeIn Ignition. This app gives you control of your computer, from anywhere you can connect to the web.

Setup is easy – install the app, then download and install the free client software on the computers you want to access. In the Ignition app, log in with your email address and password: you now control all the computers associated with your LogMeIn account.

It's not as easy to use your computer via a mobile device as it is from a desktop keyboard. Getting used to the mouse is tricky: you move it with a finger. To open or close a window on the remote desktop you must pan so that the icon is positioned under the mouse pointer, then double-tap on the screen. You can limit the remote computer's screen size, resolution and colour quality to save bandwidth, and specify whether your network is a LAN or internet connection. During tests, we had no trouble at all remotely using various computers on the default settings.

As apps go it's not cheap, but we're smitten with LogMeIn Ignition. It's easy to install and use. The app makes remote access of your desktop PC simple to such an extent that it makes your Android device as useful a laptop. An essential purchase for all business-focused Android owners.

Documents to Go 3.0

★★★★ $29.99

Dataviz Documents To Go has a long pedigree. It's been seen on smartphones from Palm and BlackBerry for years in lieu of a native document viewer, and is fast becoming the productivity app of choice on Android too. If the one selling point of boring old Windows Mobile phones was their support for Word and Excel, Dataviz bridges that gap. The free version lets you view word processor files, spreadsheets, presentations and PDFs and use the on-screen keyboard or a tab/toggle approach to navigate and update entries.

The full $29.99 edition offers equivalent document types (Word To Go, Sheet To Go, Slideshow To Go and PDF To Go) that can import, edit and save versions of your files locally and even recalculate formulae. Formatting is preserved and there's support for documents on SD Card. A menu of recently opened files helps find the one you want. If you need to edit documents, this is a powerful solution – but the full app is expensive, and for many users a simple eBook or PDF viewer may perform many of the functions offered here.

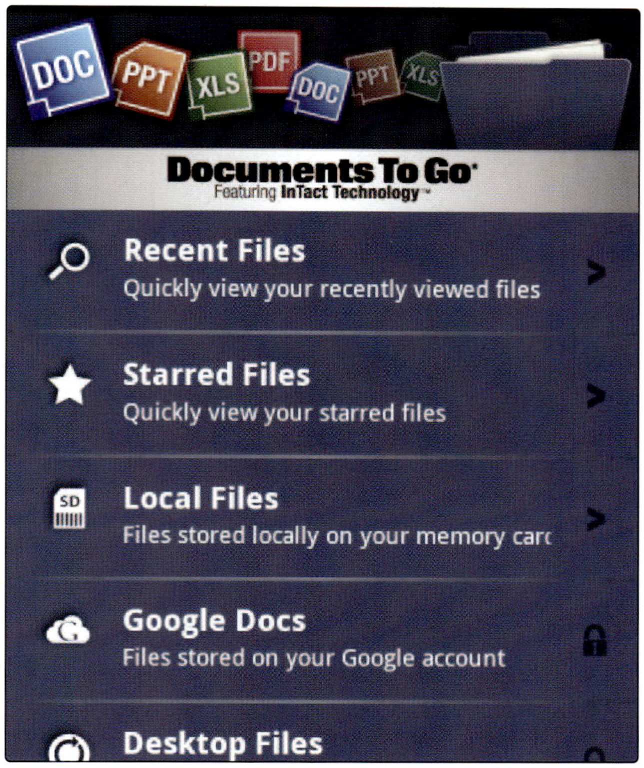

dgQuickCut

★★★★ FREE

If technicians who work on Android all day recommend it, you know this is a decent app. It lets you create shortcuts – icons that can launch an app or perform various functions – on the desktop or in the notification tray; the latter are referred to as 'dropcuts' because they appear only in the drop-down menu you get when you expand the notification area.

You can generate a dropcut from almost any action in any app, as well as many more that aren't easily found within the Android OS. For example, we access the Battery History option only by adding it to our dropcuts. You will appreciate the ability to add and change shortcuts; we're always accidentally hitting the default Search combo. The possibilities are as numerous as the apps you use.

Evernote

★★★☆☆ FREE

Evernote is a comprehensive note-taking application that integrates hardware, software and other apps. It captures text notes, voice notes, photos or files and stores them online for easy retrieval.

On Android, setup involves creating an account – your Google email is the default, but you can specify another – and deciding between creating a new note or snapshot or viewing existing ones. Once you've got a few notes, the Search and Tag options begin to come into their own.

One of the most useful elements of Evernote's Premium and desktop versions is its built-in Web Clipper. The clips can be viewed on your Android device and sorted according to tag. The developers suggest recipe clips, for example.

LIMITED CLIP

Within the free version of Evernote for Android, however, your actions are limited to viewing and organising what you've saved. For many tasks, you either need to go Premium ($5 per month or $45 per year) or revert to using the free desktop version. An Android tablet edition would provide the best of both worlds.

There's a lot to be said for the simplicity of the concept. The home page features a search bar and four buttons, each for a different type of data capture. To access your Notes, Pending Notes and Settings or to log out, you hit the Menu key. You can label your Notes with custom tags or GPS geotags and search by either, and organise Notes into folder-like Notebooks. The search function is a bit fussy if you don't have the note tagged correctly.

Optical character recognition (OCR) is one of Evernote's best features. It can recognise, index and search printed and handwritten text within photos – useful for capturing business cards, organising contacts or taking notes at meetings.

However, Evernote can't store notes on your device, only in the cloud, so if you have no web access you're stuck. Photos and voice notes need to be downloaded every time you want them. This is a versatile app, but it's limited by the need to use it online and with the desktop app and browser add-on.

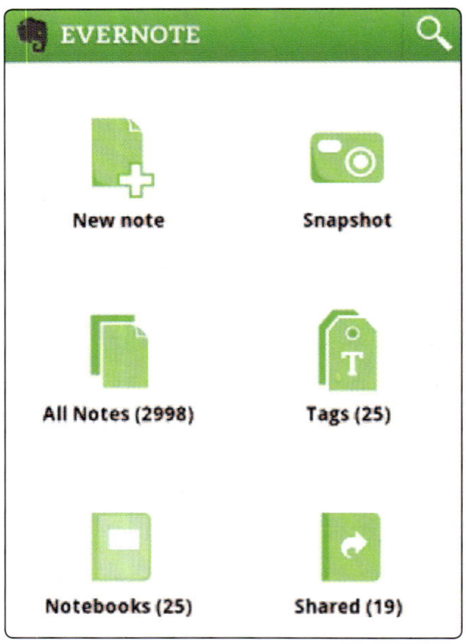

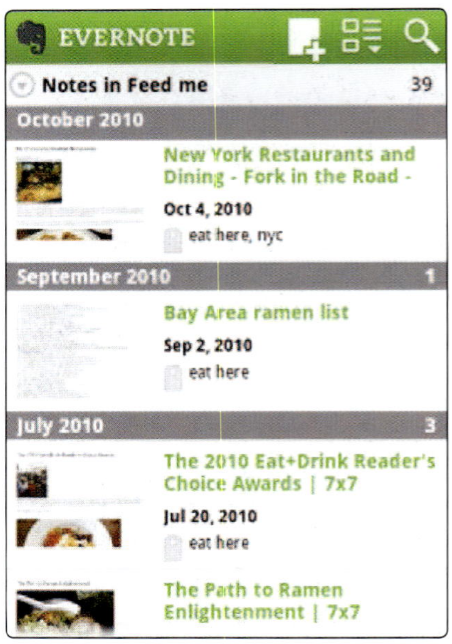

WaveSecure

FREE

The jury is still out on how susceptible smartphones are to viruses and other forms of attack, but it's wise to lock your device just in case. While a worm or other web- or email-bound nasty may pose a threat to the data stored on your handset, it's far more likely that your personal files, email logs, PayPal or credit card details will be vulnerable when someone steals the hardware. While you can probably cope with someone 'borrowing' your phone and posting a cheeky Facebook update in your name, it's a more serious issue if strangers are able to get at your emails and find out personal information.

WaveSecure adds peace of mind by locking your Android device, making its contents inaccessible. Remote data wiping is supported on some newer Android models, but this app deserves credit for being free and easy to use.

As one user wrote in wry appreciation of this app: "I bought a Nexus One on Craigslist. It was stolen – he got it back."

SplashID

£6.12

SplashID acts as a universal, secure data-storage utility for web user accounts and passwords, birthdays and other data. It keeps a password file on your Android device that's encrypted with the 256bit Blowfish algorithm, one of the most secure (and speedy) available.

Having set a master password, you create accounts, grouped under categories such as 'Serial Numbers' and classified as Business, Personal or Unfiled, with a choice of 55 custom icons for easy identification at a glance. Each entry can have a URL, username, password and several customisable items.

The desktop version lets you wirelessly sync your info with a Mac or PC, which saves you bashing away at the onscreen keyboard and gives you a non-mobile backup of your passwords and other important data should you lose your handset. It's a shame wireless sync isn't an entirely automatic process, and requires you to know the IP address of your computer. But that won't be a big hurdle for most users.

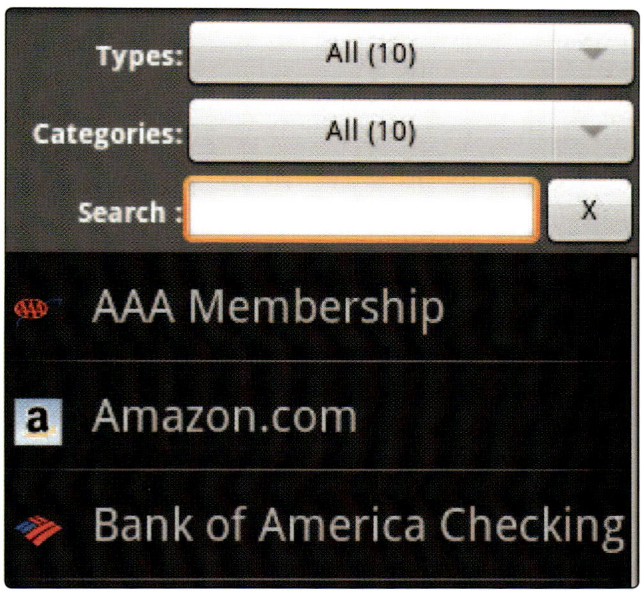

Norton Mobile Security

FREE

One of the first places people often turn to when searching for antivirus protection for their new computer is Symantec's Norton suite of security tools. The company is now looking to extend that protection beyond the PC to your mobile phone through its Norton Mobile Security app. A standalone beta version is available for free. It adds an extra layer of protection to your phone well above just having a lock screen.

SECRET PASSPHRASE

With the Norton Mobile Security app, you set up a secret passphrase and select "buddies" either from your phone book or by manually entering the number. Phone numbers on that buddy list can then send a text to your phone along with your passphrase to either lock down your phone, or in extreme cases, wipe both the phone memory and SD card. So if your phone was ever stolen, a simple text would render it useless to the would-be thief. Also available is an option to lock down your SIM card.

The app runs continuously in the background and can be scheduled to perform malware scans as desired. In addition, Norton scans each app that you download to make sure it will not harm your phone. The malware parameters can be updated manually or set on a schedule in the same way as the malware scans.

Another feature is the call and SMS blocker. You can choose to block someone from your call log, or (if you have a friend who keeps bothering you) someone from your phone book. The app can also suppress notifications: you can still see the text in the messaging app but you won't be notified of receiving it.

Even with the app running in the background, we experienced no slowdown or loss of battery life on our Motorola Milestone. Despite its beta status, this app has the look and feel of a premium app. Be sure to download and try this excellent security app now while it's free.

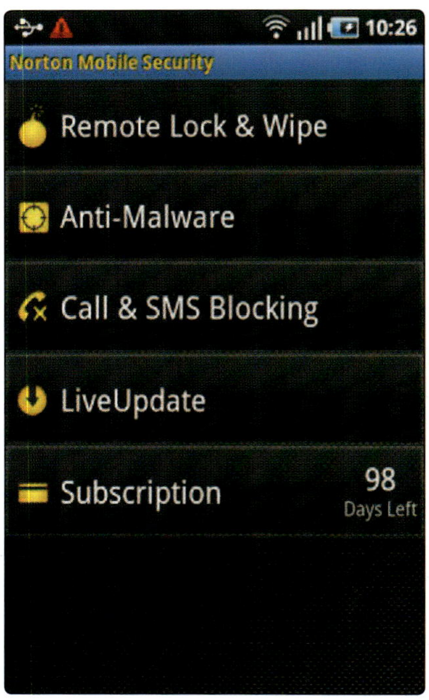

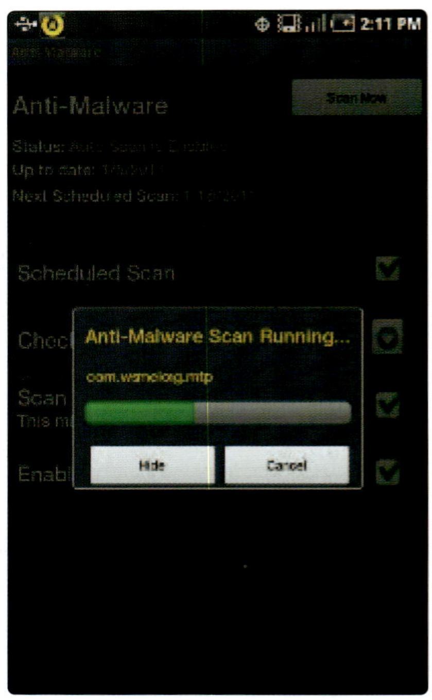

Location-based services

Pintail

★★★★½ FREE

Pintail is an app for finding lost Android phones. When you send an SMS message to yourself from another phone, containing your chosen personal identification number, Pintail texts you back with the location of your device. It's that simple. Setup is easy: type a four-digit PIN into Pintail, close the app and you're done.

You can now text 'Locate ####' to your phone from anywhere, and within a few minutes it will text you back its location details and a link to Google Maps. It's real a lifesaver if you happen to leave your phone in a cab or at a café. For what it does, this app is a great freebie.

Foursquare

★★★½ FREE

Most location-based services just give you information. Foursquare adds a competitive edge to being in the right place at the right time by rewarding you with badges for 'checking in'. Visit often enough and you can become the 'mayor', ousting the previous most regular customer.

Many venues offer discounts for Foursquare users to tempt you to buy their goods rather than a rival's. Becoming friends with other people via the service is also part of the fun, and you can then message each other. Tell Twitter or Facebook you've checked in somewhere with a 4sq.com location link and you can tip others off about the best bars, restaurants and events in your neighbourhood.

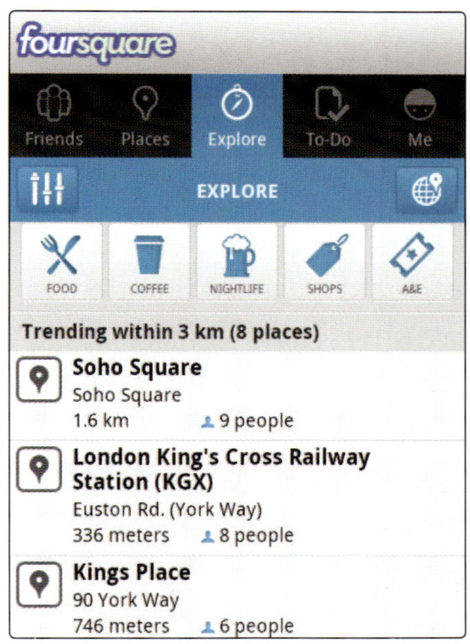

Google Maps Navigation

★★★★☆ **FREE**

The Google Maps Navigation app builds on Google Maps, which already comes as part of the Android OS, by giving users visual and audio turn-by-turn directions from their current location (using GPS) to a new destination. The app is easy to use: once you've chosen to drive or walk, simply enter your destination. You can enter a street name, postcode, or even type of place, such as 'restaurant' or 'Post Office', as your destination.

Once your handset's GPS has identified your location, which can take anything from a few seconds to over a minute depending on signal strength, the route is calculated. A blue icon is displayed on the map at your current location, with a blue line marking the route the software has created.

You can also view step-by-step instruction as a list. Meanwhile, a female voice offers an audio version of the instructions. We loved the range of customisation options, from being able to turn off the audio navigation to switching between 3D satellite maps, street view and standard Google maps. Because the app uses a web connection to obtain the latest maps, users will never need a printed map as long as they are connected.

There are some negative points though. Unlike many satnavs, the app gives you the same estimated journey time no matter what the time of day. For example, it calculated 39 minutes for a journey from King's Cross to the Kent/London borders – achievable in the early morning perhaps, but unrealistic during rush hour. In fact, the only indication of how congested your route is comes from Google's Traffic View, which colours roads in green, yellow, or red based on how busy they are.

Google Maps Navigation is a useful app. It works well, and as it's free, it's excellent value for money too. If you don't want to invest in a satnav, Google Maps Navigation is a worthy download.

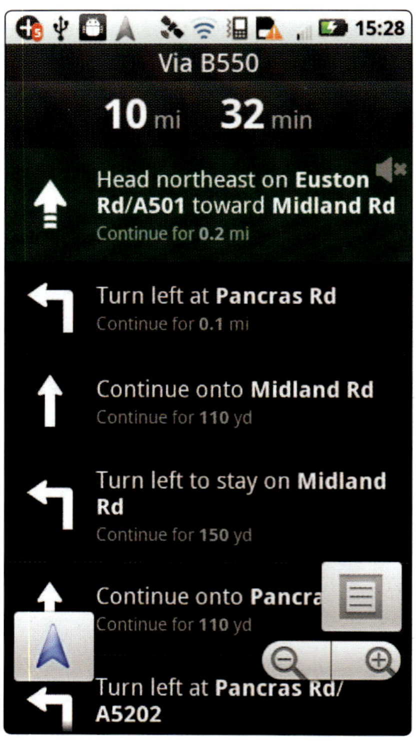

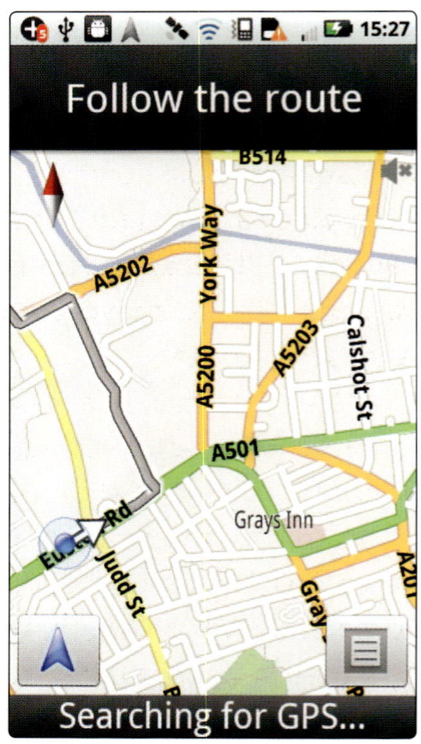

Games

Angry Birds

★★★★☆ FREE

Beware! Load Angry Birds onto your phone and your productivity will be shot. Your significant other will feel overlooked, your children will cry for your attention; you, meanwhile, will be blissfully unaware of anything except an intense desire to fling cute-looking birds at cartoon pigs.

Now available on Android, Angry Birds is one of the most popular iOS games of all time – and with good reason. It's clever, it's entertaining, it's absorbing and it proves that a great game need not be overly complex to master.

The game is simplicity itself. Birds are loaded onto a slingshot, which you pull back with your finger. They are then flung at pigs, who protect themselves via a variety of complex fortifications. You can change the slingshot's angle and how much you pull it back. When you fling a new bird, you can see the trajectory of the previous one, so you have an idea of what angle to use.

You begin with small red birds, but as the game progresses you unlock new ones with different abilities. For example, one bird drops eggs that explode on impact, while another can smash right through wooden obstacles. As the fortifications around the pigs become stronger and more complex, you'll need to develop strategies for breaking through and destroying those pesky pigs.

The animation is smooth and pinching to zoom in and out looks cool. The game did hang on us occasionally, but your progress is always saved.

The app is supported by ads, which can be intrusive; but a paid-for option is planned to let users remove these. The upshot? If you're a gamer, you'll want Angry Birds, and even if you're not you'll still want it.

Pirates & Traders

★★★★ FREE

Anyone who has played Sid Meier's Pirates should feel right at home with Pirates & Traders, an open-ended game in which you sail around the Caribbean seas in search of wealth and glory.

You start off by choosing a name, your nationality (British, Dutch, French or Spanish), some skill points (sailing, fencing, charisma, and cunning), the type of ship you want, and the difficulty setting. You also have some options for adjusting when the autosave kicks in.

When you begin playing, you'll find that there's loads of information to take in. Fortunately, no matter what screen you are on, you can always consult the help menu, which explains all the data on the screen, as well as what you can do. It will still be a lot to absorb at first, but at least it will be a less daunting task.

While sailing the seas you will come across other ships, and how you engage them is up to you. When you arrive at ports, you can meet with the governor, trade with merchants, buy and repair ships, or go to the bank to put away money for retirement. That last step becomes crucial, since you age in Pirates & Traders and eventually your skills will begin to decline. Learning when to retire is something of an art.

Pirates & Traders is a fun, addictive game that has a lot going for it. If this title is representative of where gaming is headed for the Android platform, then Android users will have a lot to celebrate in the coming months.

Speed Forge 3D

£1.76

Speed Forge 3D for Android is a fun racing game that gives you six different locations in outer space to race through.

The game takes advantage of the accelerometer in your smartphone and provides plenty of feedback as you crash. We found ourselves squealing with delight when we tried out Speed Forge 3D and experienced our initial wipeouts. When you smack into something you don't just get the odd knock along the way, but a plethora of explosions and a wildly vibrating handset.

Once you've got the hang of things, the competitive element kicks in. You are in effect in a time trial against other racers and are encouraged to get them off your tail by hurling mines and missiles in their direction. Of course, they are just as likely to try the same trick with you. However, since these aren't real racers in the online gaming sense, their reactions are just that – a shame, given the obvious potential and excitement garnered by the graphics and environment.

FAST AND FURIOUS

Speed Forge 3D offers much better graphics and vehicle handling than on some games we've seen before. The faster Snapdragon processors and larger-screens that Android handsets offer confer an advantage here. The 3D effects are surprisingly good and we found ourselves getting thoroughly into the action. What's lacking, though is the ability to play against other people. You can charge around the preset scenes at breakneck speed and won't upset the physics engine that handles the graphics. But perhaps, like space itself, the world of Speed Forge feels barren and lonely.

N.O.V.A.

★★★★☆ £3

N.O.V.A. has taken gaming on Android to a whole new level, with captivating graphics, awesome first-person shooter action, and even online death matches. You'll be slaughtering aliens in a range of areas; N.O.V.A. features 13 levels spread throughout five distinct environments. Your arsenal is also fairly robust: six weapons are available to you including a handgun, shotgun and rocket launcher. Aside from just blasting aliens, you'll get to man turrets on the ground or on the back of a jeep, solve small puzzles that unlock ammo boxes, battle bosses, and more.

As you progress through the game, you'll unlock special abilities like freezing enemies or increased run speed. N.O.V.A. plays and feels like a complete console game. You can even play in online death matches of up to four people via Gameloft Live.

On the screen, there's a life meter and buttons for weapon selection, reload, grenades, pause, music, special abilities, jump, move and aim. When it comes to the controls, you have a few options. The default has a virtual joy stick for movement and a button for firing while looking around and aiming is done by dragging anywhere on the screen. The controls are very responsive and you can adjust the sensitivity to your liking.

N.O.V.A. has stunning graphics, and everything is highly detailed – from intense space battles to lush landscapes full of atmosphere. The sound effects and music are top notch, too.

PES 2011

★★★★½ £1.83

Install PES on an Android device and you can get your footie fix wherever you are. Lacking the corporate sheen of the officially sanctioned FIFA games but with a much more realistic games engine, Konami's Pro Evolution Soccer has long been the choice of serious soccer fans on the console. Following a transfer to the iOS with the 2010 version, PES 2011 is now available from the Android Market.

STRENGTH AND DEPTH

As ever the strength of PES is the gameplay. Despite the restriction of having to use a virtual controller via your device's touchscreen, PES feels like the rarest of things: a fully featured mobile game. It takes a while to get to grips with tackling and heading (as it should), and goals are tough to come by, but with some practice you'll feel immersed in as realistic a football sim as you can find.

The learning curve is relatively steep, but the standard required of newbies is far from frightening. Load the game and quick-start into a match and all but the most digitally challenged will be able to compete from the off. More importantly, when you're playing against the AI – as you will almost always be on a mobile device – it is sufficiently intelligent. Sometimes we found the player changes frustratingly difficult to second guess, but this has always been a criticism of Pro Evo, and with practice you get used to it.

Stadia and pitches are designed and rendered beautifully, and we like the way the pitches change to suit 'overhead conditions'. And far from the days where every Dutch player was known simply as 'Oranges', PES now has details of oodles of top European teams, with officially licensed UEFA Champions League and UEFA Europa League modes (obviously you'll play the reserves in the latter).

The graphics are excellent, the options myriad and the scope for self improvement plentiful. Playing on a smaller screen will make you pine for your console on occasion, but for mobile gaming there's simply no better footie option than PES 2011.

Soccer Superstars

£3.06

Soccer Superstars is an Android game that strikes the right balance between depth and casual fun to appeal to anyone who's a fan of the sport. Featuring retro graphics and music reminiscent of Nintendo's 8bit NES, Soccer Superstars is a charming soccer game with RPG elements.

The game has several gameplay modes, ranging from cultivating the talents of an individual player to being the manager of a team, to picking a team and taking it on to the pitch.

The controls are easy to master, and a quick tutorial guides you through the basics of how to play. As a result, you get started right away, rather than struggling with a complicated control scheme. And even though the controls are simple, a lot of strategy is involved in gauging when to pass, when to shoot and so on. Since the game retains the rules of football, fouls and penalties apply. Luckily, the help section does a good job of explaining these points to novice players.

Avid football fans will enjoy playing the manager mode. Here you have various options for tweaking and improving your team's statistics as you play through various tournaments and international friendly matches, trade players, and make various other changes.

Although the formations you can create for your team are limited, you at least get to decide whether to play attacking, defensive or balanced play – combining these features creates a wider array of strategic possibilities.

Overall, Soccer Superstars strikes the right balance between appealing to diehard fans of the sport and attracting casual gamers. It's easy to recommend this to anyone interested in playing a soccer (or football, even) video game.

Android phones

Chapter 6

Chapter 6
Android phones

The smartphone market has exploded in recent years and Android phones are leading the way when it comes to choice. Indeed, there are so many different models to choose from that finding the right one can be a daunting task. So we've picked the cream of the crop, ranging from the latest high-end models to more affordable options. >

Google
Nexus S

The Android-based Nexus S is the second Google-branded smartphone to hit the market, succeeding the Google Nexus One. It's also the first handset to run version 2.3 (Gingerbread) of Android. The mobile operating system is getting smoother and the Nexus S is an excellent smartphone, but it brings little new to the table.

It has an entirely plastic body. The gloss-black finish gives it a sleek look and feel, while a slightly contoured display sits comfortably on your cheek when making calls. Although it doesn't feel flimsy, the Nexus S has a toy-like resemblance when compared with handsets such as the iPhone 4 and even its Nexus One predecessor. The design is close to the Samsung Galaxy S, which is unsurprising since the Nexus S is also made by Samsung.

At 4in, it has a larger display than its predecessor, and the super AmoLED screen is bright and vibrant. Four neat hardware buttons at the bottom of the display take you to the Home screen and allow you to search or bring up settings, but you'll find yourself enamoured with the 3D scrolling effect of the main display and you'll happily trawl through its menus.

Used with the iPlayer app, the bright screen and Flash support make a compelling case for watching movies and TV shows on a smartphone.

NEW FEATURES

One feature that marks out the Nexus S and Gingerbread OS is its support for near-field communications (NFC). In its infancy in Europe, it's an established technology in the Far East and Google expects it to become a de facto contactless payment method.

Other new features in Android 2.3 are best described as refinements rather than revolutionary. A revamped keyboard, better copy-and-paste functionality, improved power management and a slicker user interface all figure. Text entry and editing are also more efficient than with previous Google Android handsets.

Gingerbread's new user interface is slick and smooth, and the darker colour menus and notifications give the Google Nexus S a much more professional

look. The main menu has a cool scrolling 3D effect, and the new 'TV off' screen-lock animation looks superb.

We experienced a number of crashes during testing; our review unit turned itself off on more than one occasion daily, suggesting that Google still has kinks to iron out.

Battery life has improved, with our review unit lasting more than a full day with Wi-Fi and auto-sync switched on. As with all Android phones, the software is customisable with third-party apps from the Android Market.

PICTURE PERFECT

The lack of a digital zoom is frustrating as the Nexus S' 5Mp camera takes reasonably good photos. The camera's user interface has a nice variety of settings that you can tweak to your liking, such as autofocus, macro and infinity modes, four resolutions to choose from, nine scene settings, three colour modes, three quality modes, and exposure metering.

Google's handset also has a front-facing camera for making video calls or taking self-portraits. You can shoot video as high as 720x480 pixels at 30 frames per second. A video that we shot outdoors looked pretty good, if a bit jittery when a fast-moving object went by. Colours were accurate and details were fairly sharp.

VERDICT

We can see why Google chose the Samsung handset design to show off its Gingerbread 2.3 OS – unlike the many HTC and LG devices, it's distinctive. It also features a large, colourful screen and NFC capability, while the improved interface bring it closer to the iPhone. Judged against the stunning Desire HD, however, the Nexus is unable to convince us of its supremacy.

Details

★★★★☆

Price £30/month
Further information www.google.com/phone/detail/nexus-s
Specifications Google Android 2.3 (Gingerbread); 3.8in, 480x800-pixel display; 1GHz Cortex A8 Hummingbird processor; 5Mp (rear), VGA (front) camera; 16GB memory; 3G, HSDPA; 129g; 63x11x124mm

HTC Incredible S

The HTC Incredible S is an 8Mp cameraphone that costs £30 per month on a 24-month contract. Launched as an Android 2.2.1 smartphone, HTC says that its over-the-air upgrade to Gingerbread 2.3 will be "before the end of May".

The very bright 4in Super LCD screen has a widescreen resolution of 800x480 pixels – ideal for video playback or video chat. The solid 8Mp main camera credentials are joined by a 1.3Mp camera on the rear and 720p video capture.

POWER RANGER

These run off a 1GHz processor and 768MB of RAM, and there's a powerful 1450mAh battery too. HTC claims 580 minutes of talktime on GSM, but despite some app and connectivity management, we still found ourselves needing to recharge this handset within 24 hours.

The camera has a flash, digital zoom and autofocus, which we were impressed to find was able to focus in effectively just 2 or 3cm from an object. The lens isn't straight-through, though, so you aren't actually shooting what's right in front of your eyes.

Photo effects can be set in advance or applied post-shot. Colour options include sepia, vintage, bleak and overexposed, while there's a distortion fish-eye lens effect and a vignette plus solarise and posterise effects.

FRIENDS REUNITED

Other smartphones offer unified messaging and the ability to tweet to friends on several social networks at once, but few do it with as much panache as HTC handsets. FriendStream lets you go straight to your Facebook, Flickr or Twitter account and get or post updates to each or any. The useful URL shortener will win over inveterate twitterers.

Another solidly executed feature is that for media sharing via the Connected Media app. This offers a simple way of showing off your handset-produced media content. You can share your Facebook photos with it too.

Another impressive element relates to call handling. Click the usefully large Phone lozenge at the bottom of the screen and you're immediately shown a list of recent callers and their phone

numbers. Smart Dial allows you to sort through lengthy contact lists by initial characters or numbers.

Finally, there's solid web browsing and a highly accurate G-Sensor and digital compass that swiftly pinpointed our location and orientation.

VERDICT

If you going to call something Incredible, it should perform feats previously thought impossible. The HTC does nothing of the sort, but there's still plenty to like and we were charmed by the attention to detail paid to how the average user might get more from their device.

Details

★★★½☆

Price £30/month
Further information www.htc.com/uk/product/incredibles/overview.html
Specifications Google Android 2.2.1; 4in 480x800-pixel display; 1GHz processor; 8Mp camera (1.3Mp secondary camera); 768MB RAM, 1GB internal memory; Wi-Fi b/g/n; 136g; 120x64x12mm

HTC **Wildfire S**

With its sombre grey finish and squarish design, you might easily mistake the HTC Wildfire for an old-school Windows Mobile phone. Turn it on, however, and you'll find an Android device that offers a very enjoyable user experience.

The screen resolution is limited to a basic 320x480 pixels, but the Wildfire makes up for this with the vibrance of its display and its superb responsiveness. We like the unfussiness of this phone's interface. Casually sweep a finger down its screen to unlock it and you can dive straight into the most commonly accessed features. Each of the Wildfire's large icons is clearly labelled.

You can access photos from a media card or over Wi-Fi and upload them straight to the built-in Flickr and Facebook apps. A Gallery button lets you view Facebook and Flickr updates, while the Friend Stream lets you keep on top of what's happening on the social front.

The same kind of simplicity applies to web browsing. Press the internet icon to navigate directly to any site you like. You can also pinch to zoom in and out.

The seven-screen setup works well and keeps the core phone functionality front and centre, exactly where it belongs. Click the large Phone button and your contacts list pops up. Tap a name and you get a choice: immediately call the number listed as their primary contact, or view details of their other numbers, addresses and email listings associated with them.

INSTANT REACTION

The responsiveness of the Wildfire's touchscreen is striking. Haptic feedback (the subtle feeling that you're actually touching things) is minimal, but you can see the action you initiated has been noted when the nippy processor gets to work straight away.

You can share Android apps as well as media over email, by text message or on Facebook or Flickr. Photos from the 5Mp camera can be uploaded straight to any social media site, too.

One of our favourite features is Flashlight. This easy-to-find app (bottom left on the App screen) simply illuminates whatever's in the vicinity – dropped keys or your travelcard, for example. This is a neat touch that shows just how much thought has gone into this mid-range Android Gingerbread phone.

VERDICT

The HTC Wildfire S is lighter and sleeker than first appearances suggest. It may be a fairly inexpensive Android phone, but there's more than enough here to keep most people entertained, connected and informed. The responsive touchscreen and the newer Android 2.3 OS give it a slight edge over the cheaper LG Optimus.

Details

★★★★☆

Price (SIM-free) £229 inc VAT
Further information www.htc.com/uk/product/wildfires/overview.html
Specifications Google Android 2.3 (Gingerbread); 3.2in, 320x480-pixel screen; 600MHz processor; 5Mp camera; 512MB ROM/512MB RAM; 3G, HSDPA; 105g; 59x12x101mm

Motorola **Atrix**

The Atrix is a smartphone equipped with a 1GHz dual-core processor. It runs Google's Android 'Froyo' 2.2 operating system, has an HDMI-out port and records HD video.

Motorola's powerful HD Multimedia Dock (below) and Laptop Dock accessories attempt to make it more than just a smartphone, but this is a fast and powerful mobile device in its own right, and is a worthy choice for anyone looking for an excellent all-round Android phone.

The Atrix is less than 11mm thick, which is a nice surprise given that it comes with a large 4in capacitive touchscreen. Motorola has used 'Gorilla Glass' for the display, which the company claims is difficult to scratch or crack. The screen is bright and clear and has excellent resolution, but its text is a little smaller than on most other Android smartphones, and it doesn't fare too well in bright sunlight. The display has a resolution of 540x960, making it a full 16:9 screen that's great for video playback.

The Atrix has four touch-sensitive buttons that sit below the display. These menu, home, back and search keys are backlit and generally responsive, but they are easy to accidentally bump. They also can't be used to wake the Atrix when the screen is locked.

FINGERPRINT READER

Along with external volume controls on the right side, the only other physical button on the Motorola Atrix is a power/ lock key that also doubles as a fingerprint reader. This worked relatively well during testing, but is slower than using a pass code or pattern unlock option.

The Atrix uses Android 2.2, which supports Flash and has the ability to act as a wireless hotspot. While it should be able to run version 2.3, since it has a dual-core processor and very high-end specs, Motorola hasn't announced whether this handset will receive this update.

The device comes with the latest version of Motorola's Motoblur service. This is a widget-based interface that combines multiple social networking and communications accounts, such as Facebook, Twitter, Last.fm and Yahoo Mail. You'll

need to create a Motoblur account to use the Atrix, but it's free and all content and data is pushed live to the handset.

We like the idea of Motoblur, however, the execution of the service on previous smartphones was far from perfect. Some of the flaws we encountered with the early version of Motoblur have been corrected though, including the ability to resize home screen widgets.

The handset also features Swype text entry with the on-screen keyboard. This allows you to slide your fingers over the letters you want to type in a single motion, letting the software work out the word you're trying to write. Though it sounds awkward, Swype is very easy to pick up and surprisingly accurate. As with most on-screen keyboards, the software will learn as you type and add words that you use regularly to its database.

FAST MOVER

It's one of the fastest Android phones we've tested. Swiping through home screens and using multitouch gestures is smooth and efficient, while the web browser renders pages quickly, and didn't suffer when loading Flash-intense sites. The Atrix has a few handy applications preloaded, including Quickoffice, Media Share (for playing video and music through a DLNA-compatible television) and task, battery and data managers.

VERDICT

The Motorola Atrix doesn't stray too far from the norm once you look past its dual-core processor and fingerprint reader, but it's a slick, super-fast Android phone. Anyone after a new Google Android phone with a big screen should definitely consider this handset; we just hope that Motorola gives Atrix users the latest Android updates.

Details

★★★★☆

Price £TBC

Further information
www.motorola.com/atrix

Specifications Google Android 2.2 (Froyo); 4in, 540x960-pixel screen; 1GHz dual-core ARM Cortex A9 processor; 5Mp camera; 1GB RAM; 3G, Bluetooth, Wi-Fi 802.11b/g/n; 135g; 64x10x118mm

Samsung **Galaxy S II**

Samsung's Galaxy S Android smartphone (reviewed on page 144) won PC Advisor's Best Buy award last year and it's not hard to see why. A slim, lightweight and very nippy handset with an amazing super AmoLED screen, the distinctive-looking phone was one of the best Android mobiles of 2010, and one of the few serious rivals to the iPhone 4.

Samsung's highly anticipated follow up, the Galaxy S II is one of the very first Gingerbread Android 2.3 smartphones, so we were intrigued to see how it compared.

We were also intrigued to find Samsung has completely redesigned the hardware, putting clear blue water between it and the original design (and subsequently adopted by Google for its own Nexus S Gingerbread 2.3 phone). The all-new Galaxy S II is quite angular. This enables it to accommodate a marginally larger 4.3in touchscreen (the original had a 4in display), but with no change to the 480x800-pixel resolution. The new model looks superficially similar to the HTC Incredible S (reviewed on page 122).

The build quality, if anything, has been improved upon. It's still a plastic chassis, but the handset now feels more rigid. Samsung has also upgraded the screen material to tough Gorilla Glass.

PLEASURE TO USE

Usability and navigation are as joyous an experience as on the first Galaxy S. The hyper-real brightness of the screen is still a real wow and though the overall handset design is not as strikingly different as its forerunner, the S II's 4.3in display feels far more expansive.

The internal memory now comes in a choice of 16GB or 32GB capacities and there's a faster dual-core 1.2GHz ARM Cortex A9 processor. The original Galaxy S' 3Mp camera gets a mighty bump to 8Mp and there's now support for 1080p video playback at 30 frames per second. It's quite simply a joy to use.

The original Galaxy S was already a fast smartphone, but this latest version feels even faster. We found it provided a near seamless navigation experience

when flicking between different applications, multi-tasking – even when we put it through data heavy tasks such as streaming high-definition content.

The web browsing experience isn't much changed with Android 2.3 Gingerbread under the hood. However, it offers native Flash support and an updated version of Google Maps. As with all 2.x versions of Android, you can download and open from the Android Market.

SLEEK AND STYLISH

The display is bereft of hardware buttons except the mini USB, power button, headphone and volume, putting the microSD slot inside. That helps the Samsung Galaxy S II keep its svelte and sleek feel, while Samsung relies on two touch buttons with one context sensitive big button in between.

It uses the same TouchWiz interface, which kicks in on the very speedy boot up. This retains the same colour-coded touch buttons at the bottom, with access to the most standard apps.

For navigating the internet you can choose to use the gyroscope sensor and accelerometer to enhance touch browsing. This felt a bit gimmicky, but we did love the Galaxy S II's excellent virtual qwerty keyboard.

VERDICT

Samsung has yet to announce a price yet, though SIM-free costs of £500 are suggested online. This puts the Galaxy S II firmly in the premium smartphone camp, but given the success of the first model and the impressive hardware and build quality, we expect it to find favour with plenty of Android fans.

Details

★★★★☆

Price £TBA

Further information
www.samsung.co.uk

Specifications Google Android 2.3 (Gingerbread), 4.3in 480x800-pixel screen, 1.2GHz ARM Cortex A9 processor, microSD card slot; 16GB/32GB memory; 116g; 125.3x66.1x8.5mm

Acer **Liquid Metal**

The Acer Liquid Metal is a sleek glossy black smartphone. The handset features a curved design, with a hint of metal on the back, although we found this felt a bit plasticky when the phone was being held.

Chunkier than some smartphones at 14mm thick, the Acer is 116mm long, 63mm wide and weighs 135g – dimensions we found just right for fitting in the palm of your hand and comfortable for making calls, sending emails or browsing the web.

The 3.6in, 480x800-pixel touchscreen is responsive to even a light touch. Haptic feedback notified us that our commands had been registered (if you're less keen on this feature it can easily be switched off). Four touch-sensitive buttons on the front take you to the home screen, go backwards, access the menu and launch the Google Chrome web browser.

When writing emails and text messages, users have a choice of having the on-screen qwerty keyboard being displayed in either portrait or landscape mode, by simply rotating the phone.

Powered by a Qualcomm 800MHz processor, the Acer Liquid Metal was fast to open and load apps, as well as switching between different tasks.

PORTABLE HOTSPOT

Acer's handset runs version 2.2 of the Google Android operating system. As well as being able to turn the phone into a portable Wi-Fi hotspot that can be shared with up to eight devices, Version 2.2 also offers support for Adobe Flash Player 10.1 for smartphones. Once we'd downloaded the free Flash Player from the Android Market it was easy to view sites with embedded Flash content.

All Google Android handsets come with Chrome pre-loaded, and the Acer Liquid Metal is no exception. We had no problem surfing the internet from the device, and pinch-to-zoom

means that it's easy to read text-heavy sites.

The handset also features a 5Mp camera. With a little help from smile – and face – detection technology, taking clear and sharp shots is easy. Users will also benefit from a built-in flash and 720p video capture.

As Acer handsets tend to be aimed at business users, Documents to Go is a helpful addition. It ensures Word, Excel, PowerPoint and PDF files can be opened and viewed, although to edit these files from your mobile phone you'll need to download chargeable add-ons from the Android Market.

Alongside this the handset features a number of Acer-specific apps including SocialJogger, which combines your Facebook and Twitter feeds in one place on your home screen, and urFooz that lets you create a virtual 'look-a-like' complete with profile details and bookmarks, to post to your social networks.

The Acer Liquid Metal comes with 512MB of built-in memory, although this can be expanded with a microSD card up to 32GB in Size. Users will also benefit from a music player, the ability to turn the device into a media server so media content can be shared with others and Dolby Mobile, which claims to offer excellent quality audio when listening to movies and music on the device. We did love the fact you can shake the handset to mute alarms or switch tracks when listening to the music player.

VERDICT

The Acer Liquid Metal is a sleek and functional Android 2.2 smartphone. However, while it's a worthwhile buy for the business-minded users, the handset will also appeal to teenagers and those with a passion for social networking.

Details

★★★½☆

Price (SIM-free) £300 inc VAT
Further information mobile.acer.com/en/phones/liquid-mt
Specifications Google Android 2.2 (Froyo); 3.6in, 480x800-pixel screen; 800MHz Qualcomm processor; 5Mp camera; 512MB memory; 3G, HSDPA; 135g; 63x14x116mm

HTC
Desire HD

The successor to the popular HTC Desire Android smartphone is dominated by a huge 4.3in SLCD screen. This betters its predecessor's 3.7in and makes it the largest display of the models here. Despite the 'HD' title, the 480x800-pixel resolution remains the same as before, so the pixels aren't as invisibly tiny as those of the iPhone 4's Retina Display – but there's nothing soft or blurry about it. One update reminiscent of Apple hardware design is that, like HTC's Legend, each Desire HD is crafted from a single block of aluminium.

HIGHER CALLING

Elsewhere, the specs are unmistakably high-end. A 1GHz ARM-based 8255 Snapdragon processor runs version 2.2 of the Android OS (Froyo). The 8Mp camera provides dual-LED flash and 720p HD video recording, and you get Dolby

Mobile sound. There's a meagre 1.5GB of internal memory, but the microSD card slot supports up to 32GB, fully exploited by Froyo for both data and apps. The OS also offers built-in wireless tethering in addition to a range of other improvements.

The Desire HD is also one of the first HTC smartphones to make use of the new Sense software. Enhancements include a shorter boot-up time of just 10 seconds, cached map data for faster rendering of maps and DLNA support for connection to compatible television sets. This latter feature is also found in the Motorola handsets we tested.

You also get access to HTCSense.com, a set of desktop-based services centred on backup and security. These let you locate your phone on a map, remotely lock or wipe it, and archive contacts, texts and call history. In effect, HTC users get the choice of managing their whole mobile phone experience either from their phone or from a PC.

While some of the proprietary skins and bolt-ons offered by phone vendors may seem like gimmicks, the benefits of HTCSense are convincing. Given the regularity with which handsets get lost or stolen, it's reassuring to know that as soon as you find your mobile is missing you can forward calls and texts to another phone, send a message to the device to tell whoever finds it where to return it, or remotely delete personal data. And all the HTCSense functions can then be ported to a new phone, as long as it's an HTC.

VERDICT

There's plenty to admire in the Desire HD. With the latest Android OS, a powerful processor, great camera, huge screen and attractive aluminium case, the HTC rivals the Samsung Galaxy S as the most desirable Android phone.

Details

Price (SIM-free) £469 inc VAT
Further information www.htc.com/uk/product/desirehd/overview.html
Specifications Google Android 2.2 (Froyo); 4.3in, 480x800-pixel screen; 1GHz Qualcomm Snapdragon processor; 8Mp camera; 1.5GB memory; 3G, HSDPA; 164g; 68x12x123mm

LG
Optimus One

The LG Optimus One P500 is an affordable yet highly functional Android smartphone with a 3.2in capacitive touchscreen and Android 'Froyo' 2.2. The plastic chassis may be a little basic, but its soft, rubber-style back makes it comfortable to hold and we liked the curved edges on the top and sides.

Physical buttons below the display click reassuringly when pressed and provide decent tactility, making them easier to use than the hit-and-miss touch-sensitive keys on some handsets. The one design issue we had was with the volume controls, which are a little narrow, although well positioned. The power/screen lock key requires a forceful press.

The P500's display is not as bright as some, but has a decent 320x480-pixel resolution. The capacitive touchscreen is a cut above that of the Huawei Ideos and other budget Android phones.

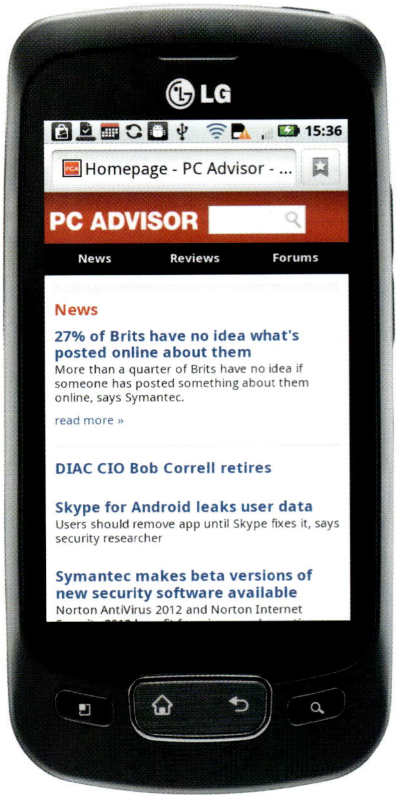

The Optimus One provides all the regular Android features and functions, including access to the Market, an excellent notifications taskbar and seamless syncing with Google services. Froyo also brings Wi-Fi tethering, the ability to store third-party apps on your microSD card and a general performance boost. The processor limitations, however, mean there's no support for Flash in web pages. In other respects web browsing is more than adequate, aided by multitouch: pinch the screen to zoom in and out. The browser also offers text reflow, so text is reformatted to fit the screen when you zoom in or out.

HOME COMFORTS

LG has skinned the Android interface with an overlay called LG Home. This offers customisable quick-access icons at the bottom of each home screen (by default Phone, Contacts, Menu, Messaging and Web) and a main menu that separates your Android default, carrier default and downloaded applications. We loved the quick toggles in the notifications drop-down for Wi-Fi, Bluetooth, GPS, 3G and silent mode; a tap of each will turn these on or off.

The on-screen keyboard supports Swype, which allows you to slide your fingers over the letters you want to type in a single motion, letting the software work out the word you're trying to write. Though it sounds awkward, Swype is easy to pick up and fairly accurate. The 3.2Mp camera takes average pictures and lacks flash. We had trouble keeping the phone steady when shooting photos and video, and even slight movement resulted in blur.

VERDICT

Overall, this is a solid Android 2.2 handset that won't break the bank and gets the essentials right, including a responsive multitouch screen.

Details

★★★½

Price £20/month
Further information www.lg.com/uk
Specifications Google Android 2.2 (Froyo); 3.2in, 320x480-pixel screen; 600MHz processor; 3Mp camera; 150MB memory; 3G, HSDPA; 116g; 109x55x16mm

Motorola **Milestone 2**

Visually, the Motorola Milestone 2 hasn't changed much from its original incarnation. It's exactly the same size and shape as the original Milestone, measuring 60x116x14mm and weighing 169g.

This sleek black-and-chrome smartphone has retained its 3.7in touchscreen display, which supports multitouch, as well as the slide-out qwerty keyboard. However, while the device might initially look the same, Motorola has made some changes for the better.

KEY POINTS

To begin with, the four-way controller on the keyboard has been ditched in favour of four cursor keys, making the other keys larger. They've been raised too.

We found the touchscreen was very responsive and needed only the lightest of touches. The keyboard keys are on the hard side, but they'll be a welcome addition for those who struggle with the size of on-screen keypads.

The Milestone 2 now features a 1GHz processor, providing a fair jump in speed compared to the original 550MHz chip. This makes the device faster at processing commands and loading software.

This Motorola runs Android 2.2 (Froyo). Among the new features supported are Adobe Flash Player and voice-to-text controls. To compose emails or text messages this way you just press the microphone icon and start speaking your message. The phone will translate your voice into text, so you don't have to worry about the accuracy of your typing.

The theoretical benefit of this facility is clear, but in practice we found voice-to-text fairly slow at translating what we said. The results weren't always a success, although that might be down to this reviewer's south London accent. While we like the feature in principle, we do think it's more suited to occasional short text messages than long emails.

The Wi-Fi implementation has been updated to ensure the handset now supports the latest standards. Motorola also gives users the ability to turn their handset into a 3G hotspot: when Wi-Fi connectivity is turned on, up to five devices can connect to the phone and access

the web through its 3G connection, network permitting.

Like its predecessor, the Milestone 2 supports microSD cards up to 32GB, but with a larger internal memory (8GB) users can get a total of 40GB. This means there's plenty of room to store pictures snapped on the phone's 5Mp camera, which comes with a dual LED flash and autofocus.

LITTLE SNAPPER

The images we captured were clear and sharp. You'll also find image stabilisation, real-time colour effects, geo-tagging, and basic in-phone editing functions such as crop and rotate. The Connected Media Player displays song lyrics and artist information for a track that's being played. There's no FM radio, but via 3G or Wi-Fi you can listen to internet radio stations.

Another neat feature that's unique to Motorola phones is Motoblur. This service, also seen on the Defy, lets you get updates from your various social networking accounts and online photo services – Facebook, Twitter, MySpace and so on – plus your Outlook email and webmail, and synchronise the lot.

VERDICT

This new model has some welcome improvements. Faster and with even more useful functions for both business and social networking, the Milestone 2 is a great Android phone. It's also built like a tank, which makes it ideal for those users who like a phone to feel indestructible.

Details

★★★½☆

Price (SIM-free) £429 inc VAT
Further information www.motorola.com/milestone2
Specifications Google Android 2.2 (Froyo); 3.7in, 480x854-pixel TFT screen; 1GHz processor; 5Mp camera; Slip-out qwerty keyboard; 8GB memory; 3G, WCDMA, GSM, Wi-Fi; 169g; 60x116x14mm

Motorola **Defy**

Motorola's Defy is a very well-built Android 2.1 handset that packs in a 3.7in display.

This screen is brighter than average and manages the clever trick of taking up almost the whole of the device's area; few smartphones have bezels as slim. We also liked the rubberised rear, which prevents the Defy getting scratched or being easily knocked off the edge of a table.

The non-slip casing extends to the sides, and as a result the protective covers for the headphone jack and charger port stick out somewhat and aren't easily pushed back into place.

ENTRY POINT

Another thoughtful inclusion is the Swype text-entry app. Compared to normal typing, this system lets you quickly pick up speed when composing messages and performing searches. When we first tried out the Defy we thought its interface was rather clunky and its cramped software keyboard a trial to use. We soon discovered that was because its default setting was expecting us to use Swype. The trick is to glide your finger from character to character rather than stabbing at each one in turn. Once you're accustomed to the scheme it makes text entry much faster.

Unified messaging, and streamlining social network access has become an important area for handset makers, so it's no surprise to find that Motorola has introduced 'Motoblur'. Rather than competing with the social network updates within Android 2.1, this proprietary social user interface adds the ability to store and easily retrieve details of those precious contacts you maintain on Facebook, Twitter, MySpace and so on.

Surfing the internet is easy. You can type in the web addresses you want to visit and when you get to your chosen site you can scroll and page-flit with ease. Support for pinch-to-zoom and a relatively responsive touchscreen help.

With 3G, A2DP Bluetooth and Wi-Fi onboard, the Defy is all set for connecting to the internet almost anywhere, and you could certainly do worse than use it for streaming audio. A Connected Music Player lets you do just this, while the excellent DNLA app

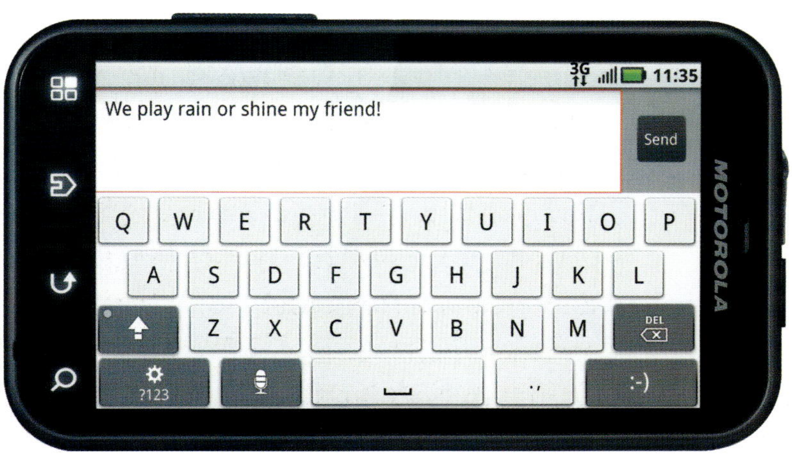

we liked so much on the Motorola Milestone 2 also makes an appearance. This lets you push music, photos and video around your wireless home network and enjoy tracks you've bought on the Defy on your home hi-fi.

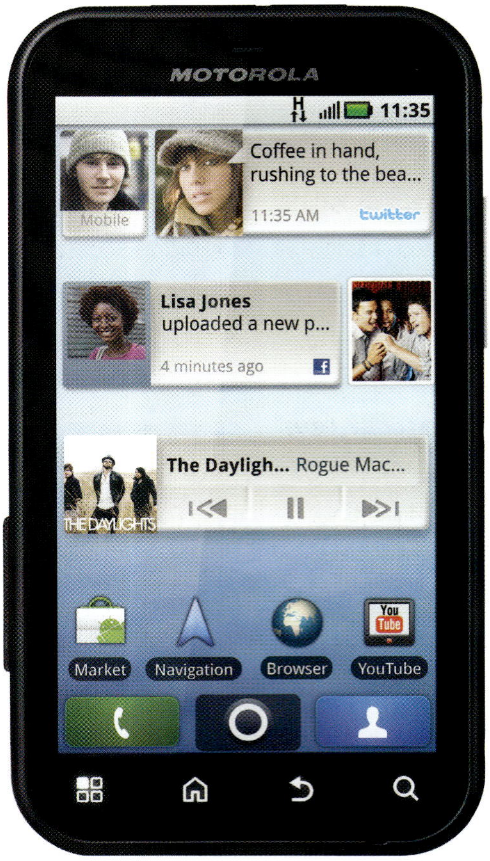

IMPERFECT IMAGE

The camera isn't quite as good as its 5Mp billing suggests. You get an LED flash and the option of tagging pictures with location data, but actually taking pictures is rather an awkward business. You need to go into the onscreen menu, as there's no hardware button to take snapshots on the outside of the handset. Nor were the shots we took anything to be proud of. Video capture is limited to VGA resolution, though viewing on the Defy is rewarding thanks to the detailed screen.

Motorola largely lets Eclair's Google apps do the talking. Google Mail, Maps, Latitude, Talk, News and Weather are all pre-loaded. Anything else can be downloaded from the Android Market and stored on the Defy's 2GB internal memory or an inserted microSD card.

A feature of note to visually impaired users is that Motorola is continuing to offer support for T3 and other hearing aid technologies along with text telephony. The Android operating system supports voice commands.

VERDICT

The engineering feat that enables the Motorola Defy to cram in a 3.7in display within its 59x107x13mm frame means you get every bit as much screen space to view web pages as you do on a fully-featured handset such as the Samsung Galaxy S. Clearly aimed at the less dainty smartphone owner, the Defy is a small but solid powerhouse that isn't afraid to take on rivals.

Details

Price (SIM-free) £279 inc VAT

Further information

www.motorola.com/defy

Specifications Google Android 2.1 (Eclair); 3.7in, 480x854-pixel screen; 1GHz Qualcomm processor; 5Mp camera; 2GB memory; 3G, HSDPA; 118g; 59x107x13mm

Acer **Stream**

Acer's smartphone line-up is split into four categories: Liquid, beTouch, neoTouch and Stream. This good-looking device is the only handset in the Stream 'series'.

It looks more upmarket than other Acer mobiles, with a tidy construction in metal-effect plastic. Be warned that the gun-metal paint is liable to chip and wear off in everyday use, however. The back is a tough rubberised plate, with a cover that slides off to reveal the removable battery and slots for the SIM and microSD cards.

The main screen is an AmoLED-type 3.7in capacitive multitouch screen. It's colourful, but not as sharp as the iPhone 4's retina display. The line of three hardware buttons below the screen is intriguing. These keys have somewhat cryptic icons, and according to the manual, they're media control buttons, to control rewind, play/pause and fast forward. We tried them on a video, but they didn't do anything. Two connection ports are offered under a rubber bung on the left edge – microUSB for charging and data connections, and mini-HDMI.

The power/standby switch is located at the top left side, where it's easy to press. Below this are volume-up and -down keys.

SAY CHEESE

On the bottom-right corner is a similar switch to activate the camera. This was tricky to operate, with no tactile feedback. Often, you would know that a picture had been shot only when it appeared on screen in place of the live view. In our tests, images were underexposed and not as good as we'd hope from a 5Mp camera.

Equipped with Google Android 2.1, this handset is somewhat behind the curve. There's no attempt to render Adobe Flash content, for instance. And we noticed that at least one key feature was absent: the option to tether the handset to a nearby laptop over Wi-Fi.

Unlocking the screen makes use of a

neat corner-roll effect, with the lower-left corner showing an animated curled page you must swipe up to unlock.

The Acer's user interface displays apps in two rows at bottom of the home screen. You'll need to swipe upwards to access the rest of the installed apps. These apps also appear at the top of the screen when you swipe sideways.

If you swipe downwards on the home screen, you can browse Cover Flow-style through recent apps and pages. Screen animations were ambitious, but a little jerky and amateurish-feeling.

Facebook, Twitter, Picasa and YouTube are built right into the Acer Stream, as well as Smart Web Radio and Google Maps.

The Acer Stream's battery life is quite good at around three days in standby, and up to two days with intermittent calls and online usage.

VERDICT

With 17 Google Android-based smartphones across Acer's four mobile phone categories, the company is taking a scattergun approach to its Android line-up. The Acer Stream is one of the better-equipped models that it offers, although there's little here to recommend this me-too handset over competitors from HTC or Motorola.

Details

★★★½☆

Price (SIM-free) £400 inc VAT
Further information mobile.acer.com/en/phones/stream
Specifications Google Android 2.1 (Eclair); 3.7in, 1GHz Qualcomm Snapdragon processor; 5Mp camera; up to 32GB Micro-SDHC card storage; 126g; 63x11x120mm

LG
Optimus Swift

Running Android 1.6 rather than the newer Gingerbread version, the LG Optimus Swift still offers plenty to entice smartphone buyers. It has a resistive, rather than capactive, touchscreen, but at just £120 this handset will win plenty of fans. It's also available in black, silver, white and pink.

INTELLIGENT DESIGN

The Swift barely tips the scales at 118g, yet its finish feels far less prone to damage than some expensive handsets. A curved insert at the very bottom of the front panel makes it easy to locate the hardware call, power and home buttons without having to look. Pressing anywhere along this strip causes these buttons to light up, while sliding a finger across from left to right unlocks the keypad.

We found the on-screen icons rather small, which is even more of an issue with a touchscreen than on a conventional display. As a result, when investigating the contents of the Apps menu we kept inadvertently launching features. However, it was easy to manage connections and to get around the settings menus using the Android button. Here you can change the wallpaper and add shortcuts and widgets, but also invoke a search or adjust settings for synchronising data and the like.

Existing contacts (but not favourites) and text messages were automatically imported into the LG's memory. The search feature narrows down the list of names you might be trying to call.

Call quality was very good, and the phone didn't get hot even after we'd been

chatting for half an hour. We noticed it juddered a little, though, as if we were triggering one of the haptic sensors.

Web surfing was an acceptable experience, even without support for multitouch pinch-and-zoom gestures. There's an incremental zoom if you need a close-up view of anything, while the clear and crisp screen ensures the text on web pages is easily legible.

AUDIO VISUAL

To take a photo using the Swift's 3Mp camera, record video or play music you'll need a microSD card, although there's 130MB of internal memory. A nice addition is the FM radio, for which you can simply plug in the supplied earphones – or better ones of your own – and press the On button before scrolling to tune in. Six channels can be selected as presets.

The LG's battery was good for more than two days of heavy-duty use, including plenty of chat and web surfing. It lasted around four to five days of more typical use. Overall, we didn't have to recharge the Swift anywhere near as frequently as an iPhone 3G for instance.

VERDICT

This is a truly likable smartphone that we'd happily recommend to friends. You'll be hard pushed to find a neater, sleeker Android phone for the price – and the long battery life is a bonus.

Details

★★★★☆

Price (SIM-free) £120 inc VAT
Further information www.lg.com/uk/mobile-phones
Specifications Google Android 1.6 (Donut); 3.in, 320x480-pixel screen; 600MHz ARM11 processor; 3Mp camera; 120MB memory; WCDMA, 3G, GSM, Wi-Fi; 118g; 55x13x109mm

Samsung **Galaxy S**

Samsung clearly had the Apple iPhone in its sights when designing the Galaxy S. The sleek candybar handset is nearly identical in size to the iPhone 3GS and mimics its chrome-trimmed black exterior. In fact, the Galaxy S is both lighter, at 119g, and has a brighter AmoLED touchscreen than Apple's alternative.

The 4in display makes colours appear vivid and bright, and it's also very responsive. Swiping to unlock the phone or answer calls soon becomes second nature, while the multi-touch support allows you to pinch to zoom in and out of web pages, maps and images. Answering a call involves a very definite swipe – again, much like the iPhone.

There's an on-screen qwerty keyboard for use when emailing or texting. It's easier to use this in landscape mode – invoked by turning the device on its side. An alphanumeric keypad can also be selected.

SOCIAL MEDIA

As an Android 2.1 (Eclair) handset the Samsung Galaxy S automatically syncs with social media accounts such as Facebook and Twitter, plus webmail

services including Yahoo, Hotmail and Gmail. Depending on the settings you specify, background data will automatically deliver updates for each of these. Such auto-syncing, however, tends to impact on the battery life.

Samsung preinstalls an eBook reader and ThinkFree Office, allowing you to view and edit documents. Also of note is the ability to play media files stored on the phone through other devices. The 8GB internal memory can be expanded with a microSD card of up to 32GB capacity. We loved the simple-to-navigate, customisable interface. A touch-sensitive button on the bottom left offers access to the Settings menu for any app you have running, while the central control button is used to exit them.

The Galaxy S has a 5Mp camera that allows you to tap the screen to define the focal point. A range of scene modes, blink-detection and anti-shake technology, plus options to add effects and adjust the exposure and white balance are all included. The resulting photos are shown off to full effect on the Galaxy S's amazing screen. The video camera, media player and FM radio are decent, but overshadowed by the camera.

The GPS location feature was quick to pinpoint our location and to accurately update as we moved from place to place. Google Maps and Google Navigation (the free Android satnav app) make use of this. We were impressed by the lack of signal problems when using 3G web access, but we wouldn't recommend overdoing it: this noticeably drains the battery. We got just over 24 hours of use between charges.

VERDICT

The Samsung Galaxy S is a great smartphone that offers a number of different features that certainly come close to rivalling Apple's iPhone. Just bear in mind that the battery may not last as long as you'd expect.

Details

★★★★½

Price (SIM-free) £439 inc VAT
Further information bit.ly/samsunggalaxy-s
Specifications Google Android 2.1 (Eclair); 4in, 480x800-pixel screen; 1GHz processor; 5Mp camera; 8GB memory; HSDPA Bluetooth + EDR; 117g; 64x13x119mm

Sony Ericsson **Xperia X10**

The Xperia X10 is an innovative Android Eclair phone with a 4in touchscreen. Its superior 8.1Mp camera was the best of those we've tested to date: it has face tracking and took clear, sharp images with vivid colour.

We found the X10's squared-off rear uncomfortable to hold for long periods, but the screen offers one of the best implementations of multitouch we've seen, responding to the lightest of touches. There's no haptic feedback, but we found the on-screen qwerty keyboard easy to use.

TIMESCAPE

The Timescape feature displays missed calls, text message previews, emails and social-networking updates as a series of ordered photo tiles, allowing you to scroll through recent activity.

The full list of software on the handset can be accessed by swiping upwards on the home screen. From here you can also access the Android Market to download apps. Press Install on the app you want and the handset will add it to your applications menu.

IMPORT DATA

The Sony Ericsson automatically imports contacts from a SIM card, preserving email addresses. You can also transfer information such as notes, your calendar and bookmarks from your old handset. Integration with social networks such as Facebook and Twitter works too, once you've logged into your own

accounts for these services.

Unique to the Xperia X10 is Mediascape, which makes your music, photos and videos accessible from one place. A MediaGo app allows for transfer between PC and handset, and the media management extends to podcasts, audiobooks and anything you access from a media card. It also works with online music stores and PlayNow.

The Xperia's 16GB internal memory can be supplemented with a microSD card up to 16GB. MediaScape also works with online music stores and the PlayNow media-streaming applet.

We were impressed with the GPS, too. The Sony Ericsson quickly and accurately located our position and faultlessly kept up when we used Wisepilot, the pre-installed navigation app.

Featuring an 8.1Mp camera with face-tracking functionality, the Xperia X10 has been aimed at photo enthusiasts. None of the other phones here has a camera of this calibre. It took clear, sharp images with vivid colours.

VERDICT

Overall, the Sony Ericsson Xperia X10 is one of the best Android handsets we've seen. It's is a stylish, feature-rich phone, making it ideal for buyers who want great photos or need to keep up to date with activities on their social media networks.

Details

★★★★☆

Price (SIM-free) £449 inc VAT

Further information www.sonyericsson.com/xperiax10

Specifications Google Android 2.1 (Eclair); 4in, 854x480-pixel screen; 1GHz processor; 8.1Mp camera; 16GB memory; HSDPA; 135g; 119x63x13mm

ZTE **Racer**

The ZTE Racer is an Android 2.1 handset that's small enough to fit in the palm of your hand. Its curved black rubber and silver plastic design looks good and the Racer is comfortable to hold when making a call or surfing the web. It's lightweight too, at just 100g.

The sleek look is complemented by touch-sensitive home, menu and back keys on the 2.8in touchscreen display. The only actual button is call/end call in the form of a long, slim silver button.

We found the on-screen qwerty keyboard slightly too small for our fingers, resulting in us hitting the wrong keys on several occasions. Using the Racer in landscape mode didn't improve the experience a great deal. When typing short text messages, we didn't mind the issue so much, but composing long emails became a frustrating process. We also had to press quite hard on the screen for our commands to be

registered. Making and receiving voice calls on the handset was easy and sounded clear.

SURF THE WEB

With 3G and Wi-Fi connectivity, the handset ensures it's easy to browse the web or check emails when on the go. However, there's no pinch to zoom. Instead you need to tap the screen to zoom in and out, which makes reading some web pages difficult.

Since the ZTE is running Android 2.1, there's no support for Flash, though the jury is out on this feature's merits anyway. Documents to Go is included as a nod to business use and allows you to open and view Word, Excel, PowerPoint and PDF files. Editing capabilities are available through chargeable add-ons that can be downloaded from the Android Market.

Entertainment is covered by an FM radio, media player and 256MB of built-in memory that can be expanded by the 2GB microSD card that comes with the device.

The phone's 3.2Mp camera offers a zoom by simply tapping the screen. There's also a handful of edits such as the ability to adjust the white balance. We found the pictures taken were relatively clear and sharp, although in some cases too much light created a halo effect on the images.

The ZTE Racer is powered by a Qualcomm 7227-1 processor, which we found to be relatively fast and responsive, without too much lag when loading apps. Meanwhile, a Skype app from 3 means users can make free Skype calls, which is sure to please talkative teenagers.

VERDICT

The ZTE Racer is a value-for-money Android handset. Aimed at occasional users, rather than those seeking a business-orientated device, it offers most of the functions associated with a smartphone but for a fraction of the cost.

Details

★★★½☆

Price £25/month
Further information threestore.three.co.uk/zte.aspx
Specifications Google Android 2.1 (Eclair); 2.8in, 240x320-pixel screen; 600MHz Qualcomm processor; 3.2Mp camera; 256MB memory; 3G, HSDPA; 100g; 55x15x102mm

Android tablets
Chapter 7

Chapter 7
Android tablets

The iPad 2 may be grabbing headlines around the globe, but its dominance in the tablet market is set to be challenged with the release of a series of Android tablets. Not only do these have the sleek good looks and usability of Apple's device, but they won't break the bank. So whatever your needs, the latest Android tablets are perfect for your mobile computing needs.

Motorola **Xoom**

All eyes are on the Motorola Xoom tablet, and for good reason – it's the first device to ship with Google's tablet-optimised Android 3.0 (Honeycomb). It also has a lot of features that set it apart from other tablets.

One drawback, however, is its price: in the UK the Motorola Xoom will be a not-insubstantial £499. While this is £80 cheaper than the comparable 32GB iPad 2 with 3G; it is still £100 more expensive than the entry-level model iPad 2 (16GB with Wi-Fi); and that's hardly considered a cheap device. We were rather hoping that the entry of Google Android to the tablet market would drive prices down, not up. But it seems Motorola has other ideas.

Still, you get your money's worth. The Motorola zooms to the top of the Android tablet class in style and design. The build quality is solid, with volume and power buttons that are easy to press.

It has a soft, rubberised feel along the top, and black metal on the bottom when held in horizontal mode. Buttons and other elements are also configured for that orientation. Clearly, Motorola designed the Xoom with landscape orientation in mind. In that position, you hold it with two hands, and the

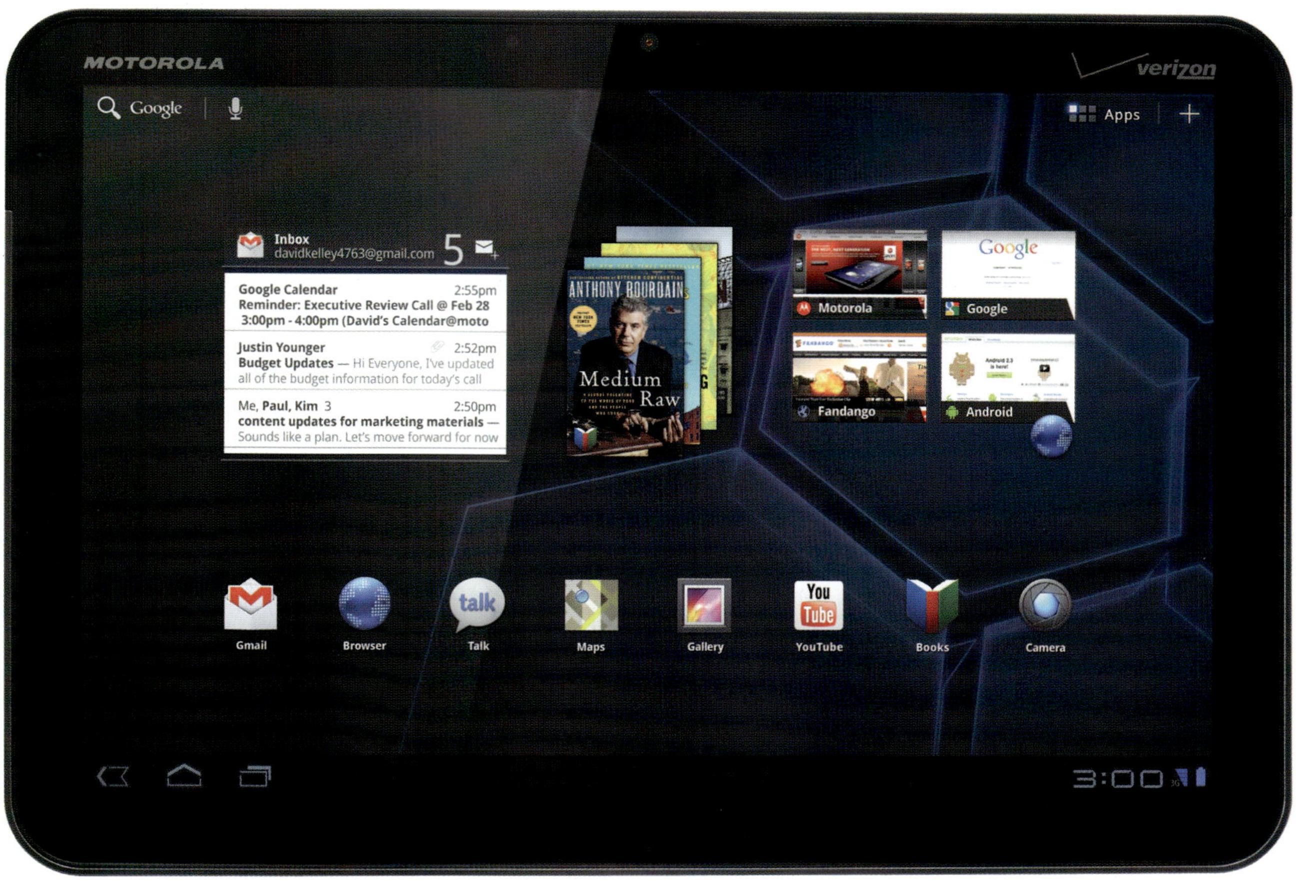

front-facing 2Mp camera sits at the top middle of the display.

The microUSB and mini-HDMI ports are at bottom, perfect for mounting the Xoom in its optional dock. The power button is located on the back too, to the left of the rear-facing, flash-equipped, 5Mp camera. It lies where your forefinger naturally lands when you hold the Motorola Xoom in both hands.

POWERFUL BEAST

There's plenty of power onboard. It uses nVidia's Tegra 2 processor, with a dual-core 1GHz processor, 1GB of RAM, and 32GB of onboard user storage. The microSD card slot permits users to double their storage space as they use the Motorola Xoom device. The display measures 10.1in diagonally, with 1280x800-pixel resolution. The widescreen's 16:10 aspect ratio makes the Xoom great for viewing video.

Initially, the display looked lovely. The home screens were readable, and colours looked fine. But as we used the device, the pattern of the screen became more obvious. Over time the Xoom seemed to present us with a grid whose lines were more obvious in some situations than in others.

The images we captured were also disappointingly middle-of-the-road. Overall, the camera was a bit awkward to operate, as was the video camera.

We were impressed with its ability to zip through content. We sped through menus, large collections of images, and the Android Market. Even the file transfer speeds via USB were impressive: we transferred 700MB of digital pictures to the Xoom in just three minutes.

VERDICT

The Motorola Xoom is a solidly built effort and Android 3.0 is easily the most polished Google operating system to date. However, there are a few flaws, such as the appearance of a grid on the screen, which prevent us from giving it a rousing endorsement. And the price feels high, given that the iPad 2's prices start at £399.

Details

★★★★☆

Price £499 inc VAT
Further information www.motorola.com/zoom
Specifications Dual-core nVidia Tegra 2 processor; Google Android 3.0 (Honeycomb); 10.1in 1280x800-pixel display; 1GB DDR2 RAM; 5Mp HD camcorder (2Mp front-facing camera included); Adobe Flash 10.1 Player support; 802.11n Wi-Fi, Bluetooth 2.1 + EDR; 32GB internal storage; HDMI 2.0,USB 2.0, 3.5mm Audio Jack; 249x168x13mm; 730g

Samsung **Galaxy Tab**

Arguably one of the closest rivals to the iPad that Android can offer, the Galaxy Tab offers the same basic features: wireless internet, a multitouch-controlled screen and a marketplace full of apps. It also has 3G as standard rather than as an option.

The most obvious difference is the 7in screen. Many people will find the smaller screen isn't a bad thing, but the 16:9 widescreen display is of a noticeably lower quality than Apple's, and the Tab itself is made of plastic, lacking the quality feel of the aluminium iPad. And while Apple's iOS interface is unsurprisingly smooth on its own hardware, Android runs rather jerkily on the Galaxy.

On the positive side, it weighs a modest 385g and is comfortable to hold. At just 12cm across, it can be gripped quite easily in one hand. Both tablets offer a similar number of pixels – 1024x768 for the iPad, 1024x600 for the Samsung – which means the Tab's are more tightly spaced. This should make it look sharper, but we weren't convinced. The duller LCD and poor viewing angles let it down.

We were impressed with the responsiveness of the Tab in core

navigation tasks such as swiping sideways on the home screen. Motion here feels smooth. Text entry via the on-screen keyboard was a bit sluggish, though, and we didn't like the clonking keypress sounds that lag just behind your finger presses.

card, available from £10/month for 100 minutes of talk time and 1GB data. Video-calling capabilities should come into their own once Skype for Android video support arrives. The Galaxy Tab has two cameras, pointing fore and aft, for the purpose.

PINCH AND PUNCH

Web browsing is acceptably fast if you've got a good 3G connection, and we found pages loaded quickly over Wi-Fi. However, pinch-to-zoom in Android is still a stuttering experience. We also spent too much time scrolling up and down pages to get to the navigation buttons.

Unlike the iPad, the Tab supports Flash, but on Flash-heavy sites you tend to get held back by the ads. We also saw some comedy lip-sync issues with YouTube videos. The YouTube app's H.264 player (also supported by iOS) is better.

One thing the iPad can't handle is phone calls. The two speakers at the bottom edge of the Tab produced fairly clear sound, and combined with a mic built into the left of the case they make it quite straightforward to use as a hands-free mobile. Call quality was easily good enough on our review sample, which came with a Three voice-and-data SIM

VERDICT

The Tab is really no match for the iPad. In its favour, it's more portable and lets you leave home without a separate mobile phone if you really want to.

Details

★★★★☆

Price £399

Further information
www.samsung.com/uk/galaxytab

Specifications 7in capacitative touchscreen; 1.06GHz processor; 1024 x 600 resolution; 3Mp camera; Android 2.2 (Froyo); GPS receiver; Microsoft Exchange support, email, voice recorder, video/audio playback; Alarm, Calculator, Calendar, Notes, Stopwatch; 802.11n, 3G, Bluetooth; phone-calling capability; 3.5mm mini-jack; 19x12x1.2cm; 385g

Dell **Streak 7**

The Dell Streak 7 is the follow-up to the company's 5in model. Although the design of the original Streak didn't impress, design is the 7's biggest asset. It's not that the new version is especially slim or stylish; rather, its build quality, button placement and subtle contours are appealing.

Even the port cover is well designed: it's sturdy but not bulky, and it smoothly fits with the edge. It provides easy access to the full-size SD card slot and the SIM card slot. The three navigation buttons – one each for back, menu, and home – are aligned at the right in landscape mode. The positioning is offset, which means your palm won't accidentally invoke the capacitive touch buttons when you're holding the device.

Regrettably, design elements alone don't guarantee a tablet's usability. For example, Dell has said that it will offer Android 3.0 on the Streak 7 in the future, but for now you get it with Android 2.2.

Unlike Samsung and its TouchWiz interface, Dell has done little in the way of customising its Android build. Everything is stock Android, except for the home screens, which have Dell's Stage user interface. Here, it provides some potentially useful home screen widgets grouped around content type (Home, Mail, Social, Music and Web, with two customisable). Mail shows

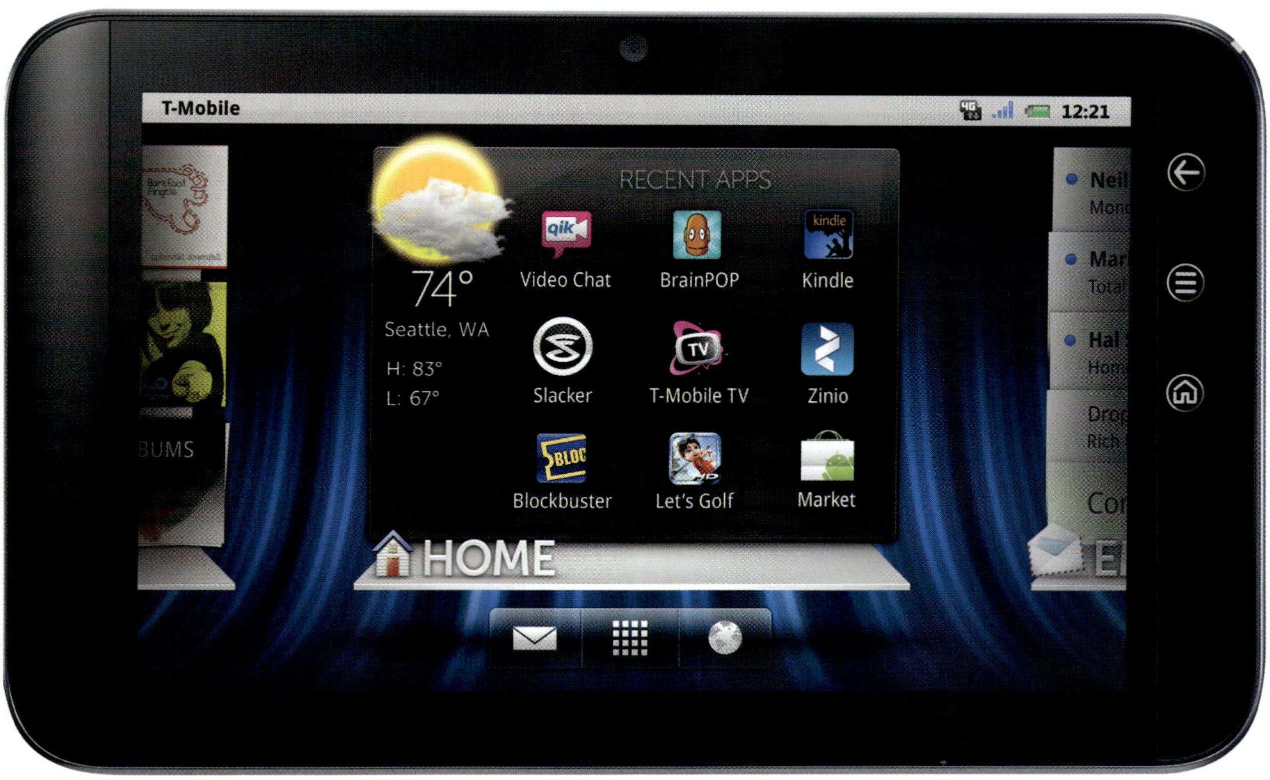

your most recent emails, while Social provides hooks into Facebook and Twitter. While appealing, the implementation leaves much to be desired, for example, the Mail widget constantly requested an email address.

The mediocre capacitive multi-touch screen is another sore spot. The 800x480 resolution display is a huge disappointment. Images looked washed out and lacked punch.

SLOW TO RESPOND

What really holds the Streak down, however, is its apparent bugginess. The screen on our test model was unresponsive on several occasions, for instance. The unit also froze when trying to open several apps downloaded from the Android Market, which could be due to bugginess in the Streak 7 or how Android 2.2 deals with those apps. But in all cases, the apps did just fine on the Galaxy Tab yet they struggled on the Dell.

The 5Mp rear-facing camera (with LED flash) also didn't live up to expectations as it felt awkward to use and produced poor quality images.

The on-screen keyboard was responsive, and conducive for two-handed thumb typing in the vertical position, but the Swipe button was often inadvertently activated when holding the device in this orientation.

VERDICT

Dell's Streak 7 counts smart design among its strengths, however, its unimpressive display and poor software implementation constrain its appeal.

Details

★★★☆☆

Price £399 inc VAT

Further information
www.dell.com/uk

Specifications Android 2.2; 1GHz dual-core T20 nVidia Tegra; HSPA + @ 2100/1900/AWS/850; 7in WVGA 800x480-pixel display; 1.3Mp front-facing camera, 5Mp rear-facing camera; H.263/H.264, 3GP, MPEG4, WMV, MP3, WMA, AAC, AAC+, eAAC+, AMR, MIDI, WAV; Full HTML WebKit browser, Adobe Flash 10.1; 16GB of internal storage; Support for up to 32GB additional storage using the user accessible SD, MMC, SDHC memory card slot; Wi-Fi 802.11b/g/n; Bluetooth 2.1 + EDR; 199.9x119.8x 12.4mm; Dell Stage 1.0; GPS; 439g

Creative **Ziio 7**

There are a growing number of tablets based on Google's Android operating system, but none has managed to hit a good balance of value for money and features. Creative might not have a background in tablets, but it knows how to build good portable mobile devices and has applied that know-how to its 7in Ziio tablet. Some specifications and features have been sacrificed to keep costs down on this Android 2.2 (Froyo) tablet, but it's still worth considering.

Our test unit came with 8GB of memory, though if you buy directly from Creative, you can get a 16GB model for £219 inc VAT.

GOOD-LOOKING DEVICE

The Ziio is nice enough to look at, even if it feels a little too plastic. Creative has kept the hardware buttons to a minimum so it doesn't interrupt the sleek finish. There's an integrated VGA camera at the top for video chats and the Ziio has a microSD card slot, one mini-USB, headphone, mic, power button and volume.

Creative made its name in the audio market and the onboard processor here allows plenty of playback tweaking. The audio quality through headphones is excellent, though the screen's resolution of only 480x800 pixels is disappointing. Some of the high-end smartphones we review here can match this.

You can get decent enough details if you stream 720p HD content to the Ziio, but the colours look washed out. The screen restrictions aren't that significant when browsing online, but the limited resolution and poor colour

palette don't lend themselves to media-rich apps. One of the issues with the display is that Creative has used a cheaper resistive touchscreen rather than the capacitive type found in most other tablets and smartphones. The screen was more responsive than we'd expected – we had no trouble navigating around the device's menus – but it's still a less fun experience.

LACK OF APPS

The Ziio uses Android 2.2, putting it in the same sphere as the far more accomplished but also more expensive Samsung Galaxy Tab. However, there's no native support for the Android Market, severely reducing the number of apps available for you to download and install. Creative has created its own ZiiStore, though this only offers only a paltry selection of apps. A big letdown.

The Ziio could also do with a feature boost. You don't get 3G on this tablet, and the Wi-Fi supports only 802.11 b/g with no support for the much faster 802.11.n. That does make streaming 720p HD content harder from a distance, but at least the 1GHz ZiiLABS ZMS-08 processor has enough power to cope with high quality video playback over a good range of formats. The Ziio also gets marks for offering a mini HDMI-out port, so you can watch your 720p video content on other displays.

VERDICT

The price is about right for this 7in tablet, but features and hardware credentials have been sacrificed. Even so, we think the Ziio is a good introduction to tablet computing and one of the better entry-level models, however, its unimpressive display and poor software implementation will limit its appeal.

Details

Price £199 inc VAT
Further information uk.creative.com
Specifications Android 2.2; 1GHz ZiiLABS ZMS-08 processor CPU; 7in 480x800-pixel display; front-facing VGA camera; H.264, MPEG4, WMV9, MOV, AVI, MKV, MP3, AAC, WMA9, FLAC, OGG, MIDI, WAV, Audible Format; 8GB internal storage; Support for up to 32GB additional storage using the microSD card slot; Wi-Fi 802.11b/g/; Bluetooth 2.1 EDR; 207x133x14mm; 415g

Advent **Vega**

With Apple dominating the tablet market, some companies just can't wait to jump in – even when their products are not ready for release. Such is the case with the Advent Vega, which at £250 appears a positive bargain next to Apple's £399 iPad 2.

It takes the same basic form as the iPad, then cheapens it in order to reduce the price tag. The resolution is comparable to the iPad's, but the Vega has a widescreen 16:9 aspect ratio. Add in its 10.1in screen size specification, and you could be forgiven for thinking you've seen this before – this is a standard-issue netbook screen with capacitive touch for fingertip control. Flip the Vega over and you'll find a plastic back, gently curved at the edges, and prone to picking up scratches when placed on the desk.

There's a flap on the right of this, which hides some useful-looking connectors. First is a microSD card slot, with Advent throwing in a 2GB card. Next to that there's an unusual full-size (Type A) USB 2.0 port – an included A-to-A USB lead in the box lets you plug the Vega into a PC, although we couldn't get it to charge from it. If you plug the Vega into a PC – Windows, Mac or Linux – you can

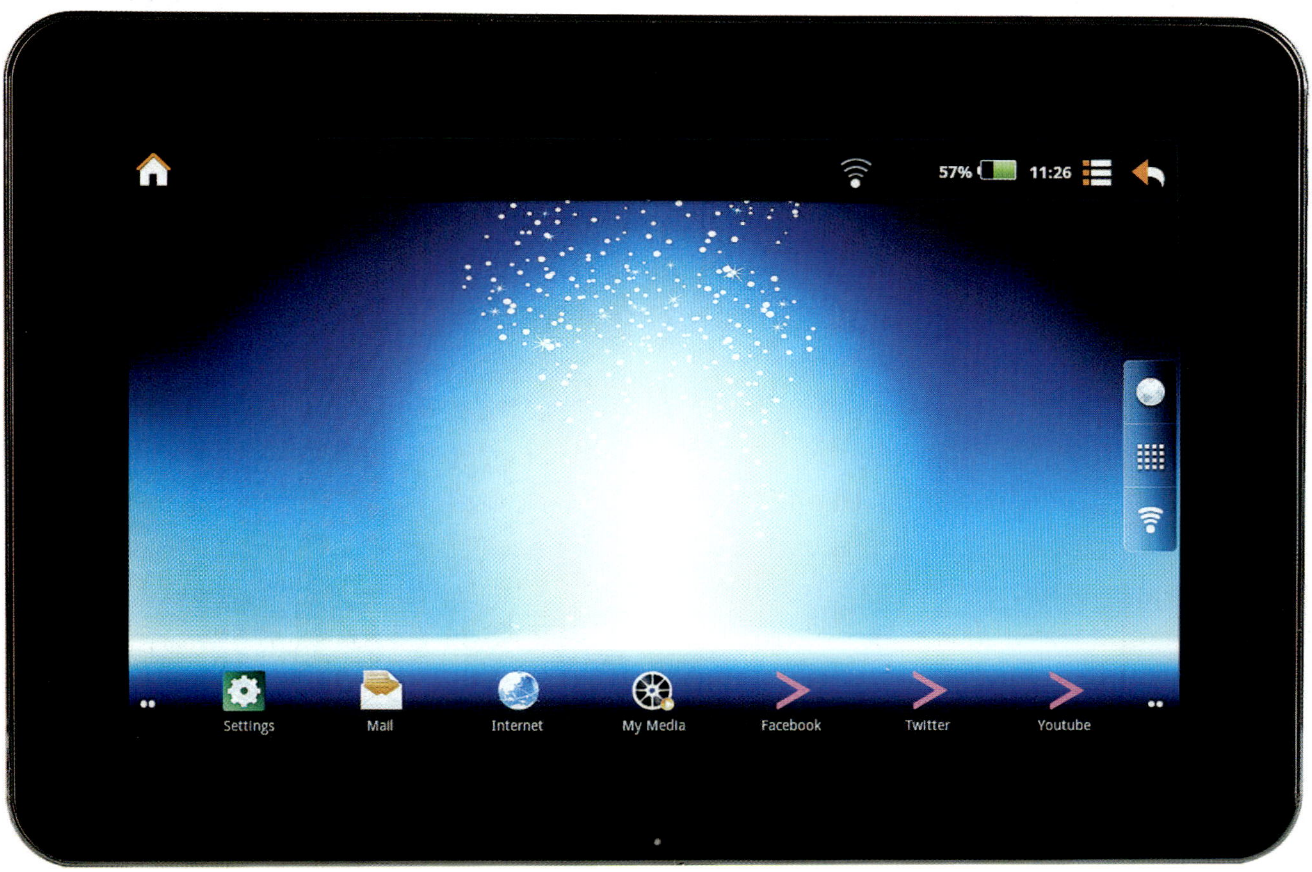

drag-and-drop music, video and photos into the relevant folders on the tablet.

The third option is HDMI. We tried connecting the Advent Vega to a monitor, and saw a mirrored version of what was on the tablet's own screen. It looked to be at the same limited resolution too, with interface elements looking very pixellated. Worse, the speed of the device slowed so much it became unusable in effect.

In contrast to most Google Android tablets, the Vega does not have the usual fixed Home and Back buttons on the front panel. Instead the Home and Back buttons are embedded within a modified version of the Android user interface, though there's a small silvered-plastic Back button on the top-right edge too.

MIXED PERFORMANCE

Some operations feel quick, like opening the web browser; others very slow and jerky, such as scrolling up and down a web page. Also, the Advent can't be used in portrait mode, as the user interface doesn't rotate when held upright.

As it's installed with Android 2.2, it has the option for a plugin to give what's called 'Flash compatibility'. In fact, Flash on every mobile device we've tried is, at best, very poor; at worse, useless. Interestingly, the designers must have known that Flash might be a problem, as they included a click-to-enable system (like Flashblock or ClickToFlash), such that you must finger-click individual Flash boxes in a web page to load content. This didn't help make Flash video any more enjoyable when it was playing, though.

Also absent is the Android Market app. Without this in place, it becomes very hard to supplement the limited number of apps already installed.

VERDICT

On the whole we have mixed feelings about devices such as the Advent Vega. On the one hand it's nice to see tablets coming down towards the £200 mark, however, too many corners have been cut. The Advent Vega has too many flaws for us to recommend it.

Details

★★☆☆☆

Price £250 inc VAT
Further information www.pcworld.co.uk/gbuk/r/advent20vega/0_0_0
Specifications 10.1in 1024x600-pixel display; 1GHz nVidia Tegra ARM Cortex A9 dual-core processor; Google Android 2.2; T20 graphics; 512MB flash storage; microSD card slot; 4GB microSD card; 802.11b/g; Bluetooth 2.1 + EDR; 1.3Mp webcam; 3.5mm mini-jack; dock connector; HDMI; USB 2.0; lithium polymer battery; 274x178 x14mm; 715g

Apple vs Google: and you win

The competition's hotting up in the race to dominate the mobile market. BlackBerry has the numbers, Apple the caché, and Microsoft has Windows – with all the familiarity that entails.

The odd one out is Google's Android operating system. More open than the rest, it can be whatever phone manufacturers want it to be. For consumers and app developers alike, inexpensive Android makes up for a lack of polish with features and adaptability. If you want a smartphone that can do more for less, Android is it.

According to ComScore, Apple's US number one status owes a lot to a massive market base of iPods. Impressive, but no more relev[illegible] to the future of mobile th[illegible] satnav sales. All the whi[illegible]ches up a greate[illegible] market share every[illegible]

[illegible]orld, Apple is in[illegible]my of Android t[illegible]g. Samsung's [illegible]berthin Galaxy Tabs [illegible] way, and the Motorola Xoom is here. High-end options are arriving each month. The iPad isn't going to struggle, but over the next couple of years it's going to have some serious, widespread competition. From Android.

Regardless of what platform you prefer, this competition is great news. Android's success forces Apple to step up its game and push out new features. Apple's success forces Google and the Android manufacturers to come up with innovative ways to differentiate their devices and offer value for consumers.

Who will win the race for mobile dominance? If you're in the market for a new mobile phone, you will.

Matt Egan
Editor, PC Advisor

JR Raphael contributed to this story